OSPREY MILITARY JOURNAL

VOLUME 2 • ISSUE 4

page 15

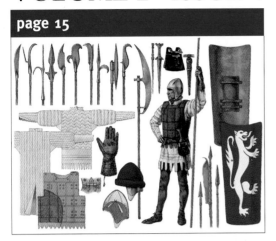

page 27

page 41

Contents

Published by Osprey Publishing Limited

All contents copyrighted © 2000 by Osprey Publishing Limited. All rights
reserved. The content of this publication may not be reproduced in any form,
printed or electronic, without prior written permission from the publisher.

Editorial
Editors: William Shepherd and Marcus Cowper

Advertising
North America: Carl A. Smith, P.O. Box 2765, Manassas VA 20108 USA
Tel: (703) 365-0159 • Fax: (703) 365-9691 • E-mail: carlsmithjr@prodigy.net
UK/Europe/International: Joanna Sharland, Osprey Publishing Ltd,
Elms Court, Chapel Way, Botley, Oxford OX2 9LP, UK
Tel: 01865 727022 • Fax: 01865 727017 • E-mail: info@ospreypublishing.com

Circulation/Distribution
North America: Osprey USA, 443 Park Avenue South,
Suite 800, New York, NY 10016, USA
Tel: (212) 685-5560 • Fax: (212) 685-5836 • E-mail: ospreyusa@aol.com
UK/Europe/International: Osprey Publishing Ltd, Elms Court,
Chapel Way, Botley, Oxford OX2 9LP, UK
Tel: 01865 727022 • Fax: 01865 727017 • E-mail: info@ospreypublishing.com

Osprey Military Journal (ISSN 1467-1379) is published bi-monthly by
Osprey Publishing Limited. Subscription rates for one year (six issues)
US & Canada $39.95 US; UK £25.50; Europe £33.50; rest of world £42.50
Periodicals postage paid.

Subscription enquiries/address changes
North America: Osprey Direct USA, PO Box 130, Sterling Hts,
MI 48311-0130 Tel: (810) 795-2763 • Fax: (810) 795-4266
E-mail: info@ospreydirectusa.com
UK/Europe/International: Osprey Direct UK, PO Box 140,
Wellingborough, Northants NN8 4ZA, UK
Tel: 01933 443863 • Fax: 01933 443849 • E-mail: info@ospreydirect.co.uk

Design: Active Designs, Oxon, UK
Origination: Grasmere Digital Imaging, Leeds, UK
Printed in the UK by Stones the Printers, Banbury, Oxon, UK

*FRONT COVER: Genoese and French crossbowmen were sent against the Prince of
Wales' position at the south-western end or right flank of the English position. A heavy
shower of rain had slackened the crossbows' string. As a result, the range of the
Genoese weapons was significantly reduced and this, coupled with a lack of pavise
shields behind which they normally reloaded their weapons, made the crossbowmen
highly vulnerable. Within a few minutes they were suffering severe casualties from the
English arrow storms and were forced to pull back. (© Copyright Osprey Publishing
from Campaign 71 Crécy 1346 by David Nicolle, artwork by Graham Turner)*

Editorial

This Issue travels the two millennia from the reign of Emperor Claudius to the
present and the battlefields of England, France, North America and the Mediterranean.
Anthony Rogers tells the story of the epic defence of Malta, also examining the
significance of other Axis strategic priorities in the ultimate survival of the George
Cross island. Moving to northern France and the battle of Crécy in 1346, Dr David
Nicolle introduces the crossbowmen of Genoa and explains the failure of the French
to make effective use of this elite force against the English longbowmen, men-at-arms
and cavalry. Two centuries on in 1513, much the same English tactics proved their
worth for the last time, against the new European method of fighting. John Barratt
describes the bloody clash at Flodden between England and Scotland, and between
two generations of warfare, bow and bill against pike. Two centuries from the
beginning of his extraordinary journey from Marengo to Waterloo it is a good time
to re-examine Napoleon's formative early years. René Chartrand looks at his
education from 1779 to 1785 as Gentleman-Cadet Bonaparte. In 1863, the American
Civil War reached its turning point at Gettysburg. General Greene's defence of Culp's
Hill was one of the most critical actions of the battle. Carl Smith tells how inspired
leadership and tactics, and heroic fighting held off numerically far superior
Confederate forces. To the present day, new evidence has led the county of Sussex to
challenge Kent's traditional claim to the beachhead for Emperor Claudius's legions.
Neil Grant reviews the archaeological, political, strategic and tactical arguments on
either side of the debate. René Chartrand, OMJ's gastronomic re-enactor, complements
this article by addressing the question of what the Roman legions ate and drank.

Marcus Cowper and William Shepherd

Malta: The Fighter Pilot's Paradise

BY ANTHONY ROGERS

Gladiators of 261 Squadron at Luqa in late 1940.

INTRODUCTION

Measuring just seventeen and a half miles by eight and a quarter, Malta is the largest of three main islands situated in the middle of the Mediterranean, south of Sicily and almost equidistant from Gibraltar to the west and Suez to the east. In 1814, Malta joined the British Empire, serving as an ideal base for the Royal Navy, the Army and, more than a century later, the Royal Air Force.

On 10 June 1940, Italy entered the war against Britain and France. At dawn the next day, the Regia Aeronautica's 2a Squadra Aerea commenced operations against Malta as 18 Macchi C.200s escorted some 55 Savoia Marchetti S.79s across the 60 miles of sea that separates the island from Sicily. Hal Far airfield, Kalafrana seaplane station and the dockyard area were all targeted. Three Gloster Sea Gladiators flown by RAF pilots intercepted the raiders in this, the first of many engagements during the next two and a half years.

The Fighter Flight's outdated biplanes were Malta's sole aerial defence for nearly two weeks following Italy's declaration of war. Eventually, they would be immortalised as *Faith*, *Hope* and *Charity* (notwithstanding the fact that there were at least four aircraft on strength with others stored in crates). On 21 June two Hurricanes, followed the next day by three more, joined the Gladiators after landing on Malta while en-route to the Middle East.

Malta had been at war for nearly two months before an operation was launched to reinforce the island's fighter force. On 2 August, 12 Hurricane Mk. Is of 418 Flight left the aircraft carrier HMS *Argus*, to be flown 380 miles to Luqa where they joined the surviving fighters to form 261 Squadron.

On 17 November, HMS *Argus* again dispatched to Malta 12 Hurricanes, this time accompanied by two Fleet Air Arm Blackburn Skuas. Tragically, eight of the RAF fighters ran out of fuel before reaching their destination, while one of the Skuas was shot down by AA fire after becoming hopelessly lost and flying over Sicily.

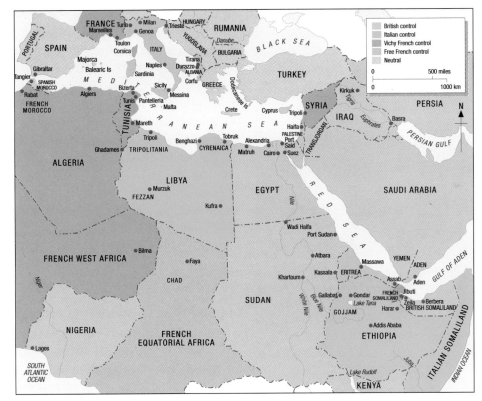

The Mediterranean theatre and Middle East theatre of war – June 1940 (© Copyright Osprey Publishing)

ARRIVAL OF THE LUFTWAFFE

Mussolini's offensive against Malta, the North African campaign and Italy's invasion of Greece finally led Hitler to send reinforcements to his ally in the Mediterranean. Towards the end of 1940, elements of X Fliegerkorps began to arrive in Sicily from Norway, and by mid-January 1941 the Luftwaffe had gathered in Sicily a formidable array of front-line aircraft. For Malta, the war was about to begin in earnest.

In January 1941, Operation Excess delivered to the island additional troops, supplies and a number of crated Hurricanes, though not without cost. The destroyer HMS *Gallant* was severely damaged by a mine, while the carrier *Illustrious* was singled out for attack by the Germans during the debut of the Luftwaffe over the central Mediterranean. After being severely damaged in a series of air attacks, HMS *Illustrious* was able to

limp into Grand Harbour during the evening of the 10th. Incredibly, the carrier was virtually ignored by the enemy until 16 January, when she was targeted by a combined force of some 44 Ju 87s and 17 Ju 88s escorted by Bf 110s, CR 42s and Macchi

C.200s. But the defenders, having learned much from previous raids by Italian dive-bombers, had prepared a formidable 'box barrage'. The attackers also had to contend with the Island's fighters, supplemented by Fulmars off *Illustrious*. Two days later, the German bombers returned, this time concentrating on the airfields at Hal Far and Luqa. On Sunday 19 January, the carrier was again subjected to a day of intensive bombing, with the attackers having to face a terrifying repetition of Thursday's barrage.

On the 23rd, *Illustrious* slipped her moorings and quietly left Grand Harbour on the first stage of her journey to the shipyards of the United States. Her remaining Fulmars stayed as welcome reinforcements for the island's air force.

Events in Libya led to the departure between January and March of a

Members of 10th Heavy Anti-Aircraft Regiment Royal Artillery with the wreckage of a Ju 87 Stuka that was probably shot down during an attack on Luqa aerodrome on 26 February 1941.

'Erks' – RAF ground crew – of 261 Squadron in 1940-41.

number of Axis aircraft from Sicily (though some Ju 88s would return in early April). Early in February, Messerschmitt Bf 109Es of 7/JG 26 were transferred from Germany to Sicily. The outstanding performance of the unit commander, Oberleutnant Joachim Müncheberg, had already gained him 23 victories and earned him the coveted Ritterkreuz (Knight's Cross).

At the end of January, six more Hurricanes arrived in Malta from North Africa. However, the Hurricane was no match for the faster, cannon equipped Messerschmitt Bf 109E. During the next four months, 7/JG 26 would claim at least 42 air victories, 20 of which were credited to Müncheberg (including one during his unit's brief involvement in the invasion of Yugoslavia) and all without a single operational loss.

Notwithstanding German efforts to neutralise Malta, the island was still able to provide the Royal Navy with a base from which to strike at Axis shipping, thus creating a constant

drain on the enemy's Mediterranean supply routes.

The island's fighter strength was sustained by the occasional reinforcements from North Africa, coupled with the constant attention of RAF ground personnel. On 3 April, Malta received its first batch of Hurricane IIAs. During the next two months there were three major Naval operations, in which the carriers *Ark Royal* and *Furious* flew off a total of 81 Hurricanes, although many were to continue to the desert after refuelling. During this time - mid 1941 - the air forces on both sides in the central Mediterranean underwent some reorganising. In Malta, a newly-reformed 185 Squadron was created with pilots from 261 Squadron, shortly before the latter unit was replaced by 249 Squadron, flown in from *Ark Royal* on 21 May. April and May also saw the arrival of the first Blenheim and Beaufighter units. In June, more Hurricanes, including the latest four-cannon IICs, were ferried in by the Royal Navy, and on the

28th, 126 Squadron was also re-formed from the recently arrived 46 Squadron to operate from Ta'Qali with 249. In July, 12 Hurricane IIs were allocated for a new night fighter unit. Malta's defences were further improved with the arrival of more troops, AA guns and ammunition.

The Allied build-up in Malta coincided with the run-down of the Luftwaffe in Sicily. Most of its aircraft were withdrawn in May for Operation Barbarossa, the German invasion of Russia. The following month, 7/JG 26 also left, flying south to Libya.

ITALIAN SEABORNE ATTACK

Tasked once again with subjugating Malta, the Italians proceeded with an audacious plan whereby they would simultaneously strike at the submarine base at Marsamxett Harbour and the recently arrived Substance convoy in neighbouring Grand Harbour. Following the withdrawal of the Luftwaffe, there had been a noticeable decrease in the number of raids. The

Ground crew of 185 Squadron at Hal Far at the height of the siege in 1942.

V7474 was one of three Hurricane Mk. Is reported missing on 26 February 1941. The pilot is believed to have been a New Zealander, Pilot Officer Charles Langdon of 261 Squadron. (© Copyright Osprey Publishing from Aircraft of the Aces 18 Hurricane Aces 1939-40 by Tony Holmes, artwork by Keith Fretwell)

Ju 87 R2 of III/StG 1, a unit that suffered considerably in its attacks on Malta in early 1941. J9+AB was normally flown by the Gruppenkommandeur, Hauptmann Helmut Mahlke. (© Copyright Osprey Publishing from Combat Aircraft 6 Junkers Ju 87 Stukageschwader of North Africa and the Mediterranean by John Weal)

Twenty four Spitfires were scrambled between 10.15am and 10.40am on Friday, 24 July 1942, to intercept five Ju 88s escorted by approximately 20 fighters. Two more Spitfires were also airborne as minesweeper cover. Three bombers and a Bf 109 were claimed destroyed by the RAF, and a number of machines probably destroyed or damaged. Amongst those involved in the action was Pilot Officer Rod Smith, a Canadian in 126 Squadron, who claimed his first aircraft destroyed when he shot down Ju 88 140247/M7+KH of KGr 806: 'We were vectored onto five JU 88s coming south at 18,000 feet. We met them at their height virtually over the centre of the island. Their fighter escort was lagging badly behind them. They were several hundred yards to our left. I was on the front left corner of our formation of eight, and therefore nearest to them. I began my 180 degree turn to port, to get behind them, slightly ahead of the rest of our pilots. I came in behind and made a port quarter attack on the one on the extreme left of their formation, which was the nearest one of course …

'I chose the port engine of the 88 to start with (a bigger target from behind than a 109 in fact) and fired a six second burst, from 250 yards closing to 150, emptying both [ammunition] drums. The port engine immediately streamed black and white smoke and caught fire, and I shifted my aim to the wing root and then the fuselage, both of which became enveloped in flames … Many pieces came off the aircraft. When I finished firing I broke violently down into a diving aileron turn to the left … When I came out of the dive I was all alone and saw the 88 coming down streaming fire and

Flt Lt Rod Smith while based at Biggin Hill in 1944

smoke in a great downward arc to the south. I then noticed a parachute high up over the centre of the island, and I could see the figure of a man in it … I was back on the ground in a mere two or three minutes, my entire sortie being logged as 20 minutes'.

The parachutist was the wireless operator, Leutnant Heinz Heuser. He was the only survivor. Those who died were the pilot, Leutnant Sepp Hörmann; observer, Obergefreiter Josef Popp; and air gunner, Unteroffizier Wolfram Quass.

islanders were therefore amazed when, during the night of 25/26 July, the Italian Navy's elite La Decima Flottiglia MAS deployed two SLC 'human torpedoes' and nine MTM explosive motor boats to a point north of Grand Harbour. Unfortunately for the Italians they were detected while still 20 miles short of their target. Furthermore, when the attack began, the SLCs failed to reach their objectives, which included the destruction of the anti-torpedo net across the harbour mouth. This task was taken over by one of the MTMs. At 4.45am, it hit and blew up the mole bridge of the breakwater causing the west span to collapse, which effectively blocked the entrance. The attack now turned into a rout for the Italians. As searchlights illuminated the scene the shore defences opened up, sending tracer rounds ricocheting off the sea into the night sky. The Italians were in a hopeless situation, made all the worse when Hurricanes took off at dawn to attack the survivors as they tried to withdraw back to Sicily. Fifteen Italians were killed in the raid, and 18 captured.

There was a sharp decline in Italian aerial activity during August and September. For the first time, Malta's forces were able to meet the enemy on an equal footing with the Navy, delivering, between July and September, seven Swordfish and 22 Hurricanes in addition to thousands of tons of supplies. The Italians did what they could to disrupt operations, but of some 67 vessels comprising the convoys

Substance and Halberd, just two ships were sunk and four damaged.

In September, several Hurricanes were fitted with Light Series bomb racks capable of holding 40lb General Purpose and 25lb incendiary bombs; the 'Hurri-bombers' subsequently carrying out a series of raids against Sicily.

On 12 November, 34 Hurricanes flown by pilots of 242 and 605 Squadrons arrived from the carriers *Argus* and *Ark Royal*. The following day, *Ark Royal* was sunk by U-81. The previous month she had also delivered one Swordfish and 11 Albacore torpedo bombers for the island's strike force.

Leutnant Hermann Neuhoff.

Spitfire Mk. V, instantly recognisable as the personal aircraft of Wing Commander Peter Prosser Hanks. The Luqa Wing Leader flew BR498 during much of the fighting in October 1942. Besides the distinctive code, this machine was unusual in lacking a tropical air filter, the removal of which marginally improved an aircraft's flight performance. (© Copyright Osprey Publishing from Aircraft of the Aces 16 Spitfire Mark V Aces 1941-45 by Dr Alfred Price, artwork by Keith Fretwell)

Late in the afternoon of Wednesday, 18 March 1942, Hurricanes and Spitfires clashed with Bf 109s escorting Ju 88s over Malta. Among the losses was Sergeant George Mulloy of 126 Squadron, who was reported missing. The victor was almost certainly Leutnant Hermann Neuhoff of 7/JG 53. After evading an attacking Spitfire, he was about to formate on the bombers when he spotted a Hurricane 100 metres below his aircraft:

'Now with the stick forward the Me dives with lightning speed towards the Tommy. He sees me coming and wants to escape. But too late, I have already pressed the buttons and my MGs and cannons bark hoarsely. He sees that there is no escape and has to engage in an air battle with me.

'Now things are really hotting up, ten times I was unable to get into position, the sweat running from my head. Then I was successful. I curved around and managed to get behind him and filled him so full of lead that he momentarily flew straight and level. It was enough – once more get him in my sights and open fire with all barrels. I was 50 metres behind that Tommy, when I saw him break up. Half of the left wing broke off, so that the bird spun twice on its own axis right in front of my nose and disappeared into the water like a U-Boat. Now one more turn around the spot, but nothing else showed. There was nothing more I could do, so I turned back and went home, in order to announce my 38th air victory to my comrades. On the return flight I met up with three more comrades, who had seen the air battle and could positively confirm the shooting down'.

Just over three weeks later, Leutnant Neuhoff was made a prisoner of a war after baling out of a battle-damaged fighter over Malta.

Messerschmit Bf 109F4 'White 2' piloted in March 1942 by Leutnant Hermann Neuhoff of 7/JG 53. (© Copyright Osprey Publishing from Aircraft of the Aces 2 Bf 109 Aces of North Africa and the Mediterranean by Jerry Scuts)

RETURN OF THE LUFTWAFFE AND THE ARRIVAL OF THE SPITFIRE

With the onset of winter, the Germans began to transfer to Sicily aircraft from the Eastern Front and elsewhere. It was the beginning of the end for the Hurricane's short-lived reign over Malta. In December, II Fliegerkorps replaced the Regia Aeronautica in day operations over the Island. German raids began on a relatively small scale, increasing in intensity towards the end of the month, with daylight bomber sorties heavily escorted by the latest Messerschmitt Bf 109Fs.

In order to survive as an Allied base, the island had continued to be re-supplied by sea, but there still remained an urgent requirement for more fighters. On 7 March, 15 Spitfire Mk. VB(Trop)s were flown in from HMS *Eagle*. At last, here was a machine with both the speed to match the Bf 109 and the firepower required to destroy the Ju 88. At about this time, 1435 Flight (formerly the Malta Night Fighter Unit) also received as a welcome addition to its own Hurricanes, four Beaufighters on detachment from 89 Squadron in Egypt.

On 21 and 29 March, Malta was reinforced with 16 more Spitfires. In the interim, the survivors of convoy MW10 reached the island. Consequently, the Luftwaffe redirected its efforts against the harbours, thereby easing the pressure on Ta'Qali which had been rendered temporarily unserviceable after attacks on 20 March. One merchantman, *Clan Campbell*, and an escorting destroyer, HMS *Southwold*, were lost. All the remaining cargo ships: *Talabot* and *Pampas* and the Commissioned Auxiliary Supply Ship *Breconshire*, the latter a veteran of the Malta run, were among those vessels sunk as a result of heavy raids on 26 March.

During March, the fighter units underwent some reorganization with 242 and 605 Squadrons being absorbed by 126 and 185. On the 27th, Hurricane IICs of 229 Squadron were transferred to Malta from North Africa, with further reinforcements arriving in April and early the

The merchantman Talabot, which took a direct hit during a raid on 26 March 1942 and had to be scuttled to prevent any flames from spreading and detonating the ammunition she had on board.

following month, when aircraft were flown in to replace those lost in the previous five weeks of combat. Due to the high attrition rate of the Hurricanes and Spitfires, the RAF was finding it increasingly difficult to meet the enemy fighters on an equal basis. The Bf 109s frequently outnumbered their opponents and sometimes encountered no aerial opposition whatsoever.

The island's strike aircraft also suffered fearful losses. Surviving machines were kept operational by all available means, with ground crews often using spares scavenged from the wrecks which littered the airfields, and frequently working through the night to service a grounded aircraft. To protect the precious aeroplanes and service vehicles, dispersal pens were constructed from sandbags, rubble, stone and earth-filled petrol

cans, and whatever else could be utilised. By the end of April, around 300 pens had been built along with 27 miles of dispersal runway. This mammoth task was achieved by civilian labour, the Navy and Air Force and as many as 3,000 soldiers at a time, who toiled under the most oppressive conditions; in the cold, mud and rain, while in constant danger of air attacks.

The bravery and fortitude of the islanders was formally recognized on 15 April 1942 by the award of the George Cross by King George VI. It was the highest honour that an appreciative British Sovereign could bestow on a community.

On 20 April, 46 Spitfires comprising 601 (County of London) and 603 (City of Edinburgh) Squadrons were flown off the American carrier USS *Wasp*. After waiting until the aircraft landed, the Germans launched the first in a series of raids against the aerodromes. Luftwaffe aircrew demonstrated their usual skill and daring, and it is due entirely to the courage and determination of Malta's defenders that relatively few aircraft were destroyed on the ground.

Late in April, the 10th Submarine Flotilla quietly left Malta for the safety of Alexandria. The submarines were not to return until the end of July. It was also at this time that reconnaissance aircraft photographed what appeared to be three airfields being levelled in Sicily. Reports indicated that these were intended for gliders for a proposed Axis invasion of Malta. Codenamed Herkules by the Germans, and C3 by the Italians, the

Grand Harbour in 1942: in the background, the merchantman Talabot, and in the foreground, a destroyer, HMS Gallant, beached after her bows were blown off by a mine.

Bomb damage at Grand Harbour.

operation was planned for that summer. Yet Herkules was destined never to materialise, with Hitler instead giving priority to his offensives in North Africa and Russia. The decision ultimately sealed the fate of Rommel's Afrikakorps, thereby effecting the course of the entire war.

By May, the Regia Aeronautica had begun to reappear over Malta during daylight hours. On the 9th, Operation Bowery culminated in the delivery of 60 Spitfires flown from USS *Wasp* and HMS *Eagle*. The new arrivals were quickly introduced to the desperate fighting conditions of Malta as the Germans and Italians timed their attacks to catch the Spitfires as they came in to land. But the defenders were ready and ground crews hurriedly re-armed and refuelled the aircraft, which were

The same scene in September 1999.

immediately taken over by experienced Malta pilots who sat strapped in the cockpits, ready to scramble. Meanwhile, enemy fighters were held at bay by the island's available Hurricanes and Spitfires.

The following day, the minelayer-cruiser HMS *Welshman* completed a lone run from Gibraltar with supplies and additional RAF ground personnel. The enemy responded with a series of concentrated attacks, countered by the magnificent efforts of the RAF and ground defences, which enabled the *Welshman* to depart later that evening. Although the odds were still stacked against Malta, the situation had changed to where the defenders could again feel that they were achieving significant results as opposed to simply disrupting the enemy's efforts.

Lascaris, at the entrance to Malta's capital, Valletta, provided many civilians with a safe haven during the siege.

ITALY RESUMES THE OFFENSIVE

By the end of May, developments in the Western Desert and on the Eastern Front again led to the departure of most Sicily-based Luftwaffe units. As in 1941, operations against Malta were left primarily to the Italians and, as before, the reduction of German aircraft in Sicily provided a temporary respite that enabled Malta to strengthen and reorganize its defences. On 18 May, HMS *Eagle* delivered another 17 Spitfires. Aircraft also arrived for the RAF's strike units. With sufficient Spitfires to hand, 229 Squadron departed for the Middle East late in May. On 3 June, 31 Spitfires took off from HMS *Eagle*. All but four reached Malta. Six days later, the carrier delivered another 32 aircraft. One of the pilots was Sergeant George Beurling, a Canadian who was subsequently assigned to 249 Squadron. 'Screwball' Beurling, as he became known, would be credited with 26 aircraft destroyed (in addition

to two Focke Wolfe 190s claimed over Europe the month before) until being shot down and wounded in October 1942.

In June, convoys Vigorous and Harpoon made a simultaneous attempt to reach Malta. After suffering heavy losses, Vigorous was aborted. With Malta-based aircraft providing air cover, the survivors of Operation Harpoon continued to battle through. Two merchantmen reached the island, as did the *Welshman* on another unescorted run.

On 21 June, Tobruk changed hands yet again, this time falling to the Deutsches Afrikakorps. Soon after, 601 Squadron departed Malta to join the hard-pressed RAF in North Africa. Meanwhile, II Fliegerkorps was bolstered by Ju 88s and Bf 109s transferred from other sectors, and the Regia Aeronautica commenced a build-up of its forces in Sicily.

July began with a renewed Axis offensive that continued unabated for two weeks. RAF losses were

alleviated when the *Eagle* delivered 31 Spitfires on the 15th, followed on the 21st by 28 more. Subsequently, 1435 Flight, previously rendered ineffective as a Hurricane unit, was reformed as a Spitfire Squadron. 229 Squadron was also reconstituted with pilots and Spitfires of 603 Squadron, which now ceased to operate as a Malta-based unit.

Although the Spitfire was vital to Malta's survival, the overall situation was still critical. On 3 August, the convoy Pedestal left Scotland on the first stage of its journey to the Mediterranean. Pedestal consisted of 14 merchantmen under Royal Navy escort. By the time the convoy reached the beleaguered island, nine cargo vessels and four warships had been sunk. Of the surviving merchantmen, the most famous was undoubtedly the Texaco oil tanker, *Ohio*. After being disabled during torpedo and bombing attacks, in which one bomber actually crashed onto her deck, the battered ship finally reached Grand Harbour on

15 August, lashed between two destroyers and with another secured to the stern as an emergency rudder.

On 17 August, 32 Spitfires were launched from HMS *Furious*. Twenty eight reached Malta. During the second half of the month, Allied attacks against Sicily increased with fighter sweeps by Spitfires, and raids by Hurri-bombers flown by RNAS pilots – until being curtailed in September due to fuel shortages. During this period there was a noticeable decline in enemy air activity, but the Axis Command was still very much concerned about the ongoing disruption of Rommel's Mediterranean supply routes, and by October the Luftwaffe had gathered in Sicily a formidable force.

THE FINAL AXIS
AIR OFFENSIVE

The final Italo-German offensive against Malta began early on 11 October. Raids were almost invariably carried out by small formations of bombers heavily escorted by fighters. After seven days, during which both sides suffered substantial losses, the enemy changed tactics, resorting instead to attacks by fighters and fighter-bombers. But it was becoming increasingly clear that Hitler had lost the opportunity of ever defeating Malta.

On 29 October, *Furious* delivered another 29 Spitfires. Meanwhile, in Egypt, a successful Allied offensive at El-Alamein was followed, on 8 November, by Anglo-American landings in French North Africa,

prompting the diversion of Axis resources from Sicily to these battle fronts. For a while, attacks on Malta continued, but never with the same tenacity as before. The main problem now was the shortage of provisions. Although the situation was alleviated somewhat by the supply runs of individual ships and submarines, it was not until 20 November 1942, that the siege was finally lifted with the arrival of all four merchantmen during Operation Stoneage.

In May 1943, the Afrikakorps surrendered in Tunisia. Two months later, Malta played a prominent role as Allied Headquarters and as a forward air base during Operation Husky – the Allied invasion of Sicily. Italy capitulated on 8 September 1943, and two days later the Italian Naval Fleet began to arrive under escort at Malta, the triumphant

Lascaris today. Kiosks border the wall where the original wartime photograph was taken (see page 9), making an exact comparison impossible.

Crewman trapped in burning wreckage of his Junkers Ju 88, shot down on the north eastern perimeter of Ta' Qali on 14 May 1942.

occasion prompting a delighted Admiral Sir Andrew Cunningham to signal the Admiralty:

'Be pleased to inform their Lordships that the Italian Battle Fleet now lies at anchor under the guns of the Fortress of Malta'.

For the heroic Maltese and all who had defended their islands, it was a fitting tribute.

SUGGESTED READING

Barnham, Denis, *One Man's Window, An illustrated account of ten weeks of war Malta, April 13th, to June 21st, 1942*, (William Kimber, 1956)

Holmes, Tony Aircraft of the Aces 18: *Hurricane Aces 1939-40* (Osprey 1998)

Johnston, Wing Commander Tim DFC, *Tattered Battlements - A Fighter Pilot's Diary*, (William Kimber, 1985)

Price, Alfred, Aircraft of the Aces 15: *Spitfire Mark V Aces 1941-45*, (Osprey, 1997)

Scutts, Jerry, Aircraft of the Aces 2: *Bf 109 Aces of North Africa and the Mediterranean*, (Osprey, 1997)

Shores, Christopher, Cull, Brian, Malizia, Nicola, *Malta: The Hurricane Years 1940-41*, (Grub Street, 1987)

Shores, Christopher, Cull, Brian, Malizia, Nicola, *Malta: The Spitfire Year 1942*, (Grub Street, 1991)

Vella, Philip, *Malta: Blitzed But Not Beaten*, (Progress Press, 1985.)

Weal John, Combat Aircraft 6: *Junkers Ju 87 Stukageschwader of North Africa and the Mediterranean* (Osprey 1998)

ABOUT THE AUTHOR

Anthony Rogers is the author of *Battle Over Malta, Aircraft Losses and Crash Sites, 1940-42*, published by Sutton.

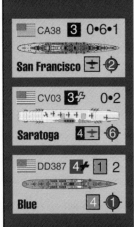

Failure of an Elite
The Genoese at Crécy

BY DAVID NICOLLE PHD

The wall-paintings in the so-called Casetta dei Soldati, in the castle overlooking the village of Avio in Italy, do not rate highly in artistic terms. But as illustrations of mid-14th-century northern Italian infantry they are unsurpassed. The paintings were made around 1340 and, though damaged, show men armed with spears, pikes, basilard dagger, large pavise shields, smaller oval shields and crossbows. (author's photograph)

The most widespread version of the battle of Crécy in the English speaking world describes the battle as a victory of steadfast English longbowmen over hopelessly outclassed Genoese crossbowmen, after which the dismounted English defeated wave after wave of overconfident French mounted knights. There is truth in this bald and oversimplified account, but what is rarely recognized is the fact that, until the battle of Crécy, Genoese crossbowmen were an internationally recognized infantry élite. How, then, did they come to fail against English infantry archers who, until Crécy, had little reputation beyond their own frontiers?

The most well-known infantry in Philip VI's army in 1346 were, of course, those Genoese. Like so many troops recruited from regions just beyond the frontiers of medieval France, they have usually been described as mercenaries. In fact this is very misleading. Most non-French troops in King Philip's army came from regions or countries which had close political or dynastic connections with the French monarchy. Genoa was an ally of France, while most of the men responsible for recruiting the famous Genoese crossbowmen, their pavesarii shield-bearers and the naval fleet in which they initially served, had long experience of serving the French crown. Nor were the Genoese ever referred to as forming companies; in other words ready-formed mercenary units. Even those mid-14th-century French units which were called companies largely stemmed from, or were recruited by, the lords of regions closely associated with the French crown.

France's weakness in archery had been recognised well before the battle of Crécy. In 1336 King Philip recruited crossbowmen in Brabant in what is now Belgium. In 1345 he tried to do the same in Aragon but from then on French recruiting agents largely concentrated on Italy, which had long been recognized as the main source of qualified crossbowmen in Europe, for service both on land and at sea. At this

A faded and smaller wall painting in the same Casetta dei Soldati in Avio Castle clearly shows crossbowmen and pavesarii acting in co-ordination, backed up by other infantry and, out of this picture, fully-armoured cavalry. (author's photograph)

PREVIOUS PAGE A battle scene painted by Altichiero, around 1375 AD, in the Chapel of St. James or St. Felix in the Santo or Cathedral of Padua. Only two crossbowmen are shown, and even they are largely hidden by the more prominent figure. By this period the status and reputation of Genoese and other northern Italian crossbowmen had declined, yet they remained an essential part of any army. It is also interesting to note that one of the infantrymen in the foreground carries a shield with the arms of the Castelbarco family, a rampant white leopard on a red ground, which was carried by many 'enemy' figures in the wall paintings of Avio Castle. (author's photograph)

time neighbouring Provençe, in what is now south-eastern France, lay within The Empire, as did Italy. To some extent it was regarded as just another part of the politically fragmented southern part of The Empire, as was most of Italy itself. Provençe was also just as significant a source of crossbowmen as was neighbouring Genoa.

Italian and Provençal crossbowmen had served in French armies since at least the early-14th century, and the so-called Genoese in French service at the time of Crécy came from many places, apart from Genoa itself. Italy and England were in fact the two parts of medieval Europe where archery played the most significant military role. But the reasons

for this were different, as were the weapons involved – crossbows and longbows respectively. Practice with the crossbow was an obligation for men throughout much of Italy, both urban and rural. Consequently there were many qualified crossbowmen around. Italy was also the most densely populated part of medieval Europe, having a notably large urban population.

The crossbow had already been responsible for a revolution in naval warfare in the 13th century, and partly as a result of this the Italians had dominated trade and warfare in the Mediterranean. They were also a force to be reckoned with in the Atlantic and northern seas. Their galleys carried large

fighting crews and these 'marines' were used as a reserve of infantry for warfare on land. In such cases the men would probably only have used their lighter crossbows, though many galleys carried both light and heavy versions of this weapon. In 1340, for example, a large Genoese galley in French service carried 40 ballistae and it was normal for there to be around 100 quarrels or arrows for each crossbow.

Though the men came from many different places, their leaders were mostly northern Italian and included individuals who had considerable military experience. The same was true of the galley captains, who were very highly paid and had been promised half the booty taken. According to the 1346-7 archives of the relatively newly-built Clos des Galées naval arsenal in Rouen, Normandy, a galley called the

Professional pavesare and his weaponry, c. 1335. Many of medieval Italy's best infantry came from mountainous regions. This figure is largely based upon the wall-paintings in the Casa dei Soldati in Avio castle between Verona and Trento. (© Copyright Osprey Publishing from Warrior 25 Italian Militiaman 1260-1392 *by David Nicolle, artwork by Christa Hook)*

A better preserved section of wall painting illustrates pavesarii in considerable detail and shows just how big their pavise shields were. The lack of such pavesarii, or at least of their mantlet-like shields, would prove disastrous for the Genoese at the battle of Crécy. (author's photograph)

Sainte Marie had as its master a certain Crestien di Grimault, a member of the famous Grimaldi family. The galley had a crew of 210 men, consisting of 1 comite, 1 souz comite, 1 clerk, 1 under clerk and 205 crossbowmen and sailors, plus the master, owner or captain. This ship left Nice in Provençe on 24 May 1346 and was contracted to serve until October (161 days) for 900 gold florins per month plus 30 florins per extra day, totalling 4,830 florins in all.

It is not clear how these men were organized when serving on land, as they clearly did, but presumably those from a single ship would remain together. Perhaps they formed the equivalent of an Italian gonfaloni urban militia unit, with their naval officer standing in for a militia officer. The ordinary gonfaloni militia unit seems, however, only to have been around 50 men, whereas a war-galley had a much larger crew. Another model could be the mercenary bandi units which were operating around places like Lucca in the 1340s. These, like a militia gonfaloni or a galley's marines, included both crossbowmen and their shield-carrying pavesarii. The latter were also sometimes referred to as spearmen, since this was their main weapon. It was used in a defensive manner, rather like a pike. Records from late-13th-century Venice refer to such weapons as being five metres long with shafts of ash or beech, and with hooks added for use at sea.

Since there were usually more than three crossbowmen for each pavesari it would seem that the crossbowmen took turns to shoot from behind the cover provided by the pavise shields or mantlets held by the pavesarii. Each man would then step back to span and load his weapon before returning to shoot. This would also have solved the problem of elbow room caused by the fact that a crossbow was held laterally while being shot. If this was in fact the Genoese crossbowmen's proper battlefield tactic, then their failure at Crécy becomes much easier to understand. Here they were clearly operating without their pavise mantlet-shields. It was traditional for Italian crossbow 'teams' to place their bows and pavises in baggage carts or on mules while on the march. At Crécy the crossbowmen had their crossbows but the pavises were indeed in the baggage waggons. Quite what the pavesarii were expected to do when the Genoese infantry were ordered forward at Crécy is unknown, though the written sources do mention spearmen advancing together with the crossbowmen.

Here it is perhaps worth mentioning that, during this period, true light infantry were not a feature of Italian armies. The famous Saracens of Lucera had been forced to convert to Christianity and had virtually disappeared from the military scene half a century earlier. The only light infantry around were a handful of Aragonese mercenaries, though there were also numerous low status ribaldi or 'ruffians.' Their role was primarily to devastate enemy agriculture rather than to fight in a battle.

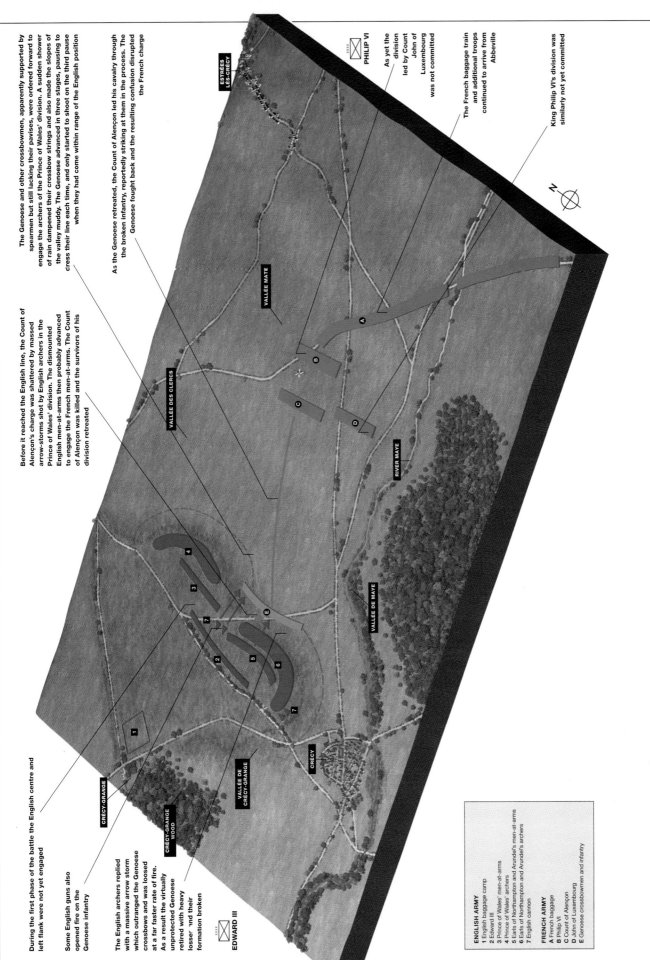

The Genoese and other crossbowmen, apparently supported by spearmen but still lacking their pavises, were ordered forward to engage the archers of the Prince of Wales' division. A sudden shower of rain dampened their crossbow strings and also made the slopes of the valley muddy. The Genoese advanced in three stages, pausing to dress their line each time, and only started to shoot on the third pause when they had come within range of the English position

As the Genoese retreated, the Count of Alençon led his cavalry through the broken infantry, reportedly striking at them in the process. The Genoese fought back and the resulting confusion disrupted the French charge

Before it reached the English line, the Count of Alençon's charge was shattered by massed arrow-storms shot by English archers in the Prince of Wales' division. The dismounted English men-at-arms then probably advanced to engage the French men-at-arms. The Count of Alençon was killed and the survivors of his division retreated

During the first phase of the battle the English centre and left flank were not yet engaged

Some English guns also opened fire on the Genoese infantry

The English archers replied with a massive arrow storm which outranged the Genoese crossbows and was loosed at a far faster rate of fire. As a result the virtually unprotected Genoese retired with heavy losses and their formation broken

ESTRÉES LÈS-CRÉCY

PHILIP VI

As yet the division led by Count John of Luxembourg was not committed

The French baggage train and additional troops continued to arrive from Abbeville

King Philip VI's division was similarly not yet committed

VALLÉE MATE

VALLÉE DES CLERCS

RIVER MAYE

VALLÉE DE MAYE

EDWARD III

CRÉCY-GRANGE

CRÉCY-GRANGE WOOD

VALLÉE DE CRÉCY-GRANGE

CRÉCY

N

THE BATTLE OF CRÉCY 26 AUGUST 1346:
defeat of the Genoese and Alençon

Another section of wall-painting in Avio Castle shows the interior of a pavise, as well as the relatively light armour worn by Italian pavesarii and crossbowmen as this time. (author's photograph)

Crossbowmen, whether Genoese or otherwise, were an essentially a static, or at least a defensive, form of infantry. King Philip's decision to send them forward against the English at Crécy, particularly as they were sent without their pavises, strongly suggests that the men in command of the French army during this battle had no real idea of how to use what were at that time regarded as the finest infantry in Christian Europe. The failure of the Genoese crossbowmen and their other infantry at Crécy was relatively brief and easily explained. They were used to forming part of disciplined and structured armies in which they would be closely supported by equally professional cavalry. Not surprisingly, therefore, the Genoese were not keen on advancing without proper preparation, without their pavises and without adequate reserves of ammunition from the supply waggons. Furthermore, they would be attacking at the end of a long day's march with the setting sun directly in their eyes. Their officers complained to the Count of Alençon, to whose battle or division they appear to have been attached, but were ignored.

So the Genoese formed up under the immediate command of Ottone Doria, probably slightly to the left of the centre of the French position, with the Prince of Wales' battle or division as their nearest target. The 2,000 to 6,000 Genoese were, of course, greatly outnumbered by the opposing English longbowmen; perhaps even being outnumbered by the closest archers in the Prince of Wales' division alone. With a sound of trumpets and drums the Genoese crossbowmen and their accompanying spearmen moved forward in three stages, each pause being signalled by a shout which would have rippled along the Genoese front as the order was passed from unit to unit. This enabled the foot soldiers to remain in formation and to adjust their dressing at each pause. Their role was to get close enough to break up the enemy line with crossbow fire, whereupon the French cavalry would charge and take advantage of any weakness in the English front. In fact, the Genoese only seem to have shot their crossbows the third time they halted, when they were about 150 metres from the Prince of Wales' battle.

Later legend recalled two great black crows which flew over the battlefield as the infantry advanced. More significant was a sudden and apparently intense shower of rain - the first in six weeks - which made the ground slippery. The bottom of the Vallée des Clercs remains very muddy, even a day after rain, for at least 250 metres from its junction with the river Maye. More importantly, the shower soaked the strings of the Genoese crossbows, making them stretch and thus lose power. The near contemporary chronicler, Jean de Venette, clearly stated that the English longbowmen took the strings from their bows and kept them dry beneath their helmets.

This painting of an opposing armed force is even more defaced, though its crossbowmen and pavesarii again form a sort of team. (author's photograph)

LEFT A final, somewhat crude drawing of the interior of a castle, just like that of Avio in which these paintings are found, also illustrates a north Italian crossbowman in his other role. Here he defends the castle from a form of strongly built wooden tower within the circuit wall. (author's photograph)

RIGHT This carving next to the south door of the church of Santa Maria Maggiore in Bergamo, northern Italy, was made by Giovanni de Campione around 1360. Again it portrays an infantryman with a large shield, perhaps a tavola rather than a pavise, and the hilt of a heavy basilard dagger. (author's photograph)

This, however, could not be done with a crossbow which required a powerful piece of machinery to be unstrung and restrung. The rain accounts for the ease with which the crude but effective longbows of the English archers outranged their opponents.

In ordinary circumstances the only advantages that a longbow had over its more sophisticated opponent was the rapidity with which it could be shot, and its ability to rain heavy arrows from high trajectory. In terms of accuracy, range and penetrating power, the advantage should have lain with the Genoese crossbows. When the Genoese did shoot they had to do so uphill with a low sun either in their eyes or slightly to their left. This was a particular disadvantage for men who aimed directly at their targets rather than dropping arrows on them in showers. As they loosed their weapons the Genoese were almost simultaneously hit by an arrow storm shot by archers in the Prince of Wales' division. A few English cannon apparently added to the noise, terror and casualties. Froissart stated that the cannon made 'two or three discharges on the Genoese' but this must mean individual shots by two or three guns since it was not possible

to reload such primitive weapons any faster. Villani, another contemporary chronicler, agreed that their impact was considerable, though he also indicated that the guns continued to fire upon French cavalry later in the battle: 'The English guns cast iron balls by means of fire ... They made a noise like thunder and caused much loss in men and horses ... The Genoese were continually hit by the archers and the gunners ... [by the end of the battle] the whole plain was covered by men struck down by arrows and cannon balls.'

Without their pavises and outranged by their opponents the Genoese infantry suffered severe losses, wavered and then streamed back. At this point they are said to have been attacked by the French cavalry who were supposedly supervising them. It is unlikely that the Genoese officers did not understand why the crossbowmen broke, but it does seem that the Count of Alençon or some of his advisors concluded that the Italians had been bribed into betraying King Philip. Again according to Jean de Venette, some French knights attacked their own infantry; 'though all the while the crossbowmen were excusing themselves with great cries.' The fact

that the English shot further volleys into this confusion suggests that the cavalry in question had been riding close behind the Genoese during their initial advance.

The idea that Philip VI would have intentionally ordered his horsemen to ride down the broken Genoese is inconceivable, as it would have ruined the momentum of the French cavalry charge – their primary battle winning tactic. Clearly, however, the men-at-arms took no care to avoid their scattered infantry and caused additional casualties as they rode over them, while some of the Genoese may have shot back with their crossbows. English archers loosed further volleys of plunging arrows into the confusion when the French came into range and many Genoese are said to have been wounded by falling horses.

Why then did the Genoese crossbowmen's own leaders agree to such a disastrous tactic, or did they have no say in the matter? One reason might lie in the relatively low status of their commanders. These were not members of the senior French nobility. Nor, in fact, were they even members of the highest echelons of the nobility of the neighbouring Empire. They may have been highly experienced and professional soldiers, but to those who commanded the French army at Crécy they were probably 'mere soldiers' and, because of their characteristic involvement in naval piracy, barely gentlemen.

Carlo Grimaldi was a member of one of the four major families in medieval Genoa, a family first recorded in the army of Emperor Frederick I in 1158 . The Grimaldis were also Guelphs, traditional supporters of the Papacy in its ancient rivalry with the Emperor. Thus, by extension, they were friends of France, which had for many years been the Pope's most powerful ally. Consequently, Grimaldis were often found in French service as mercenaries, naval commanders or allies, both within France and in the forces of the originally French Angevin rulers of southern Italy and parts of the Balkans. Carlo or Charles himself came to be known as il Grande, the Great. His father Ranieri or Rénier had been lord of the Mediterranean coastal city of Ventimiglia from 1329 to 1335 but was then ousted by a coup in favour of the Genoese Republic which was itself then dominated by Ghibbeline (pro-Imperial) families such as the Dorias. Four years later the Genoese, tired of the squabbling of their Guelphs and Ghibbeline nobility, proclaimed Simon Boccanegra as their new Doge or ruler. But even this did not lead to stability and Ventimiglia, where Carlo Grimaldi had regained control, refused to recognize the new Doge's authority. In 1341 Carlo purchased Monaco from the Spinola family and this, together with Ventimiglia and the town Roquebrune, became safe havens for Genoese Guelph families.

Meanwhile, Carlo Grimaldi and various other members of his family, friends and dependants, offered their support to King Philip VI of France in his struggle with Edward III of England. The Grimaldi's territorial power may have been tiny, but their naval potential was significant. They were also prepared, for the right price and for certain commercial privileges, to fight alongside other fleets supplied by their rivals, the pro-Ghibbeline Doria family of Genoa. Together, the Grimaldis, the Dorias, and others provided squadrons of fighting galleys and substantial numbers of professional crossbow-armed marines or infantry. These fought for King Philip VI in the Atlantic, the English Channel and in France itself. Carlo Grimaldi's powers of leadership, and perhaps his financial skills, meant that only two of his galleys deserted whereas all of Ayton Doria's did so when not properly paid in 1339.

Grimaldi galleys were back in French service from 1341 to 1343 and, for the first time in its history, the autonomy of Grimaldi-ruled Monaco was recognized. At the same time, Carlo and his brother Antonio were made vicars or governors of Provençe. The years 1345-46 were more difficult, with the Grimaldis locked in a bitter political struggle with Genoa, where they felt their family rights had been denied. In 1346 Carlo Grimaldi was temporarily ousted from Monaco by a local coup. By then, however, he was fully engaged in providing naval support to Philip VI of France, resulting in his own serious injury at the debacle of Crécy.

Carlo Grimaldi, once more the lord of Monaco and a leading entrepreneur in the recruitment of Genoese mercenaries, recovered sufficiently from his wounds to join an expedition to Majorca in 1349 in support of its deposed King James. The latter was, however, defeated and after many vicissitudes Carlo Grimaldo himself died in 1357, two months before Monaco temporarily returned to the Republic of Genoa. His son Ranieri, the lord of nearby Menton, remained a loyal servant of France, as did most of the Grimaldi family for the rest of the 14th century. The Grimaldis also regained Monaco, which Carlo's descendants rule to this day.

FURTHER READING

Allmand, C. T., *The Hundred Years War, England and France at War c.1300-c.1450* (Cambridge 1988)

Allmand, C. T., *Society at War, The Experiences of England and France during the Hundred Years War* (revised ed. Woodbridge 1998)

Ashley, W., *Edward III and his wars, 1327-1360* (1887; reprint 1993)

Barnie, J. E., *War in Medieval Society, Social Values and the Hundred Years War 1337-99* (London 1974)

Burne, A. H., *The Crécy War: A Military History of theHundred Years War from 1337 to the Peace of Bretigny 1360* (London 1955)

Contamine, P., 'Crécy (1346) et Azincourt (1415): une comparaison,' in *Divers aspects du Moyen Age in Occident; Actes du Congres tenu a Calais en Septembre 1974* (Calais 1977) 29-44

Contamine, P., *Guerre, État et Société à la Fin du Moyen Age: Etudes sur les Armées des rois de France 1337-1494* (Paris 1972)

Curry, A. and Hughes M. (eds), *Arms, Armies and Participants in the Hundred Years War* (Woodbridge 1994)

Froissart, J. (J. Jolliffe ed. and trans.), *Froissart's Chronicles* (London 1967)

Hewitt, H. J., *The Organisation of War under Edward III, 1338-62* (Manchester 1966)

Jean de Venette (J. Birdsall trans., R.A. Newhall ed.), *The Chronicle of Jean de Venette* (New York 1953)

Nicolle, David, Campaign 71 *Crécy 1346* (Osprey, 2000)

Palmer, J. J. N., (ed.), *Froissart: Historian* (Totowa NJ 1981)

Perroy, E., *The Hundred Years War* (London 1951)

Prestwich, M., *The Three Edwards: War and State in England 1272-1377* (London 1981)

Rothero, Christopher, Men-at-Arms 111: *The Armies of Crecy and Poitiers* (Osprey, 1981)

Sumption, J., *The Hundred Years War, vol. I: Trial by Battle* (London 1990)

Thompson, P. E. (ed.), *Contemporary Chronicles of the Hundred Years War* (London 1966).

Wailly, H. de, *Crécy 1346: Anatomy of a battle* (Poole 1987).

ABOUT THE AUTHOR

Dr David Nicolle worked in the BBC Arabic Service, gained an MA from the School of Oriental and Asian Studies and a PhD from Edinburgh University. He taught world and Islamic art at Yarmuk University, Jordan, and is one of Osprey's most prolific and popular authors. His latest title, Campaign 71 *Crécy 1346*, on which this article is based was published in June 2000.

Crossbowmen maintained their vital role in naval warfare, as shown in this late-14th- or even early-15th-century wall-painting of the battle of Punta Salvore by Spinello Aretino. It is in the Palazzo Pubblico of Siena and illustrates a Venetian victory over an Imperial fleet. Although the actual battle was fought two centuries earlier, the artist has portrayed it as a typical galley conflict of his own day. (author's photograph)

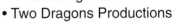

Gentleman-Cadet Napoleon Bonaparte 1779-1785

BY RENÉ CHARTRAND

Napoleon Buonaparte, the new student at the Brienne Military School, 1779. This print after a painting by Réalier-Dumas shows the young Napoleon derided by other students, an accurate description of his early days at Brienne.

Napoleon Bonaparte's childhood and education has naturally been less fully covered in the countless books and articles written about him than his later, brilliant career. Yet his early years both formed and demonstrated some of the characteristics of the genius to be.

Napoleon was the fourth child of Carlo di Buonaparte, a handsome nobleman and diplomat of the republic of Genoa who had been educated in law in Rome and Pisa. His mother, born Leticia Ramolini, was renowned for her keen intelligence and sound judgement. Napoleon narrowly missed being born Genoese. France had long sought to possess Corsica and after extensive and tortuous negotiations,

Genoa sold Corsica to France by a treaty of 15 May 1768. A significant group of Corsicans were opposed to this and some, including Carlo di Buonaparte, took up arms in open revolt against French rule. A deal had been done however, and to close it some 20,000 French troops were sent over to the island. The patriots under

Pascal Paoli were soon hemmed in and were defeated in June 1769 at Ponte Nuovo. There was almost no further opposition. The British had been sympathetic to the Corsican cause and sent some money and arms but did nothing more. Paoli fled while Carlo di Buonaparte and many others surrendered and were pardoned. French rule was benevolent and officials made real efforts to win over the fierce and proud Corsicans. It was at the end of this turbulent episode that the future emperor was born in Ajaccio on August 15 1769.

Like many Corsican noble families, the Buonapartes had modest means but great ambition. They had a degree of influence on the island as they were, by birth, amongst the elite of Corsican society. The French wanted good relations with their new wards; and for their part, many Corsican leaders felt that better relations with the French would be advantageous. The diplomatic Carlo di Buonaparte built a friendship with a General the Count de Marbeuf, military chief and administrator of Corsica, and in 1776 was sent to Versailles as a deputy of the Corsican nobility and made a judge at the tribunal in Ajaccio.

Through the 1770's his growing children's education was an increasing worry and burden for Carlo di Buonaparte. His friend General Marbeuf came up with a solution, novel for a Corsican nobleman but common enough for a French one: send Napoleon to *école militaire*, military school. This had the very real advantage of being provided for free to students qualifying for admission. If successful in his studies, the cadet would graduate to an officer's commission in the army or navy. Perhaps Marbeuf foresaw long-term benefit for France in the integration of scions of the Corsican

elite into her army. It could also be seen by the Corsicans as one of the benefits of being part of greater France. But no one could have imagined the full, eventual consequences of his suggestion, for France or for world history.

To be able to apply for admission to military school in 18th-century France, one had to come from a reasonably 'poor' but noble family. Modest means were not difficult to prove in the case of the Buonapartes. All applicants also had to produce legal papers certifying that the candidate at least 'four quarters' of noble blood. The Buonapartes could produce this evidence, but they must have wondered how a French official would react to an application from a noble family that was actually Italian. The papers verified the Buonaparte's claim to be ancient 'patricians', not only in Corsica but also in Tuscany. They submitted their application in 1776, but it generally took years for the documents to be processed with officials checking them back and forth. This called for the favour and patronage of a powerful person and, at length, General Marbeuf, whose influence was great, inquired how things were going and Napoleon was accepted at the Brienne Military School in late 1778.

NAPOLEON AT BRIENNE
Napoleon Buonaparte entered Brienne on 23 April 1779. He was nine years old and had already been at school in France, at Autun, for over three months. His parents had taken him there to learn enough basic French to get by, his native language being Italian. His education in Corsica had been haphazard and, although he was considered quite bright, the first months in the Brienne Military School were hard for him. He spoke his basic French with a heavy Italian accent and his

grammar was awful, which brought him the jeers of other cadets who felt he was a 'foreigner' of dubious nobility, although none of them came from 'grand' noble families either. Even so young, Napoleon had a will of steel which no one could sway easily and he had pride in his origins that insults could not shake. He was once caught and punished for showing scorn for a portrait of Choiseul, the minister who had added Corsica to France. Another time he was heard to state that he would liberate Corsica one day. In his pride, he avoided associating with other students and spent much time alone, reading books or just brooding. The Fathers of the Minim, the cold disciplinarians who ran Brienne, do not appear to have done much to comfort this young, alienated boy.

One student jeered at Napoleon, announcing that his father was a

Brienne Military School student Napoleon Buonaparte reading history alone in a deserted class, the shadow of his profile spreads over a map of Europe, in this very evocative composition by JOB.

By 1783 the young Napoleon had become a student leader and organized military games by building snow forts. In this print after Louis Loeb, he is shown leading an assault .

H helene petit isla

'St. Helena, small island' – from geography class notes of pupil Napoleon Bonaparte at Brienne.

commoner and a drunkard, which was, of course, totally untrue on both counts. Napoleon responded with a challenge to a duel. Alarmed at the potential consequences, the fathers punished Napoleon with solitary confinement, but did nothing to the other boy. General Marbeuf, his benefactor, happened to be at Brienne and came over to the school, had Napoleon released and looked into the Corsican child's problems. One of these appeared to be that he had less pocket money than the other students. More serious, young Napoleon, far from home and family, had no one to turn to outside the school. The kindly Marbeuf understood all this and took what he clearly perceived to be a talented and promising student under his wing. He saw to it that his allowance was adequate and, most importantly, introduced him to Madame de Brienne, the head of the town's ancient noble family. Madame de Brienne was a warm, generous, kind-hearted lady who must also have been impressed by the bright young boy, while recognizing he was only ten and far away from the tender care of his mother. From this time Napoleon spent all his leave and vacations at the De Brienne manor house and Madame became something of a second mother to him. This warmth and understanding transformed Napoleon's hitherto cheerless existence and he never forgot her kindness to him.

Napoleon did not become a social success overnight. He was still very much a loner by choice. Each cadet had a little patch of garden to cultivate and, typically, Napoleon first expanded his plot and then planted tall hedges so he could have a small private space. As time passed, the student from Corsica developed a deep interest in mathematics – which he mastered to the admiration of his tutors – geography and particularly history. Still intensely proud and wilful, the young Napoleon got into trouble now and then. On one occasion the quartermaster, a man of harsh disposition, had condemned Napoleon to the shameful punishment of wearing a rough serge coat and taking his dinner off his knees at the door of the dinning hall rather than at table. The mortification was so intolerable to Napoleon that he fell into a raging fit and was said to have had a severe nervous attack. The school principle happened to come by, relieved him of the punishment and reprimanded the quartermaster, who was scolded by the headmaster for his lack of discernment. Father Patrault, the professor of mathematics, was 'much offended in finding that his first mathematician had been treated with such marked contempt.' Things were at last looking up for young Napoleon.

Napoleon had a passion for ancient history but read from every period, devouring accounts of military campaigns. But he had little interest in languages and none at all in Latin. Quick-witted, he certainly was never at loss for quick and surprising answers, even to people who were very much his seniors. To a visiting bishop who mentioned that his name was not amongst those of the saints on the calendar, Napoleon coolly replied that 365 days were far too few for the many saints consecrated. To an examining general who asked him what he would do if he was in command of a besieged town without provisions, he retorted, 'So long as there were any in the camp of the enemy, I should never be at a great loss for a supply.'

He controlled his fiery temper better as he grew older, but without losing any of his passion. His leadership qualities were developing, but he remained, by choice, something of a recluse. Such a serious and thoughtful lad had few intimate friends. However, De Bourriene, destined to become an important politician, was amongst those few. Napoleon's sense of command and responsibility developed considerably as a teenager and he often took charge of playtime activities in the school yard. There was a

Military Schools in France

The notion of sending future officers for formal academic training in a college was relatively new in European armies. The usual course was to send an aspiring youth to a regiment in which a family member was already serving, to learn the trade as a cadet in hopes there would in time be enough money to purchase a subaltern's commission. If this type of apprenticeship had its practical merits, the uncouth habits of military camps and general lack of education were increasingly deplored in officers as the 18th century unfolded. Sciences, arts and culture were blossoming in the Age of Enlightenment all over western Europe and armies were as much affected as the society of which they were a part and were meant to protect. As a result there were various experiments in early-18th-century France and elsewhere to provide schools for specialists such as engineers and gunners.

The first true, general military school, *L'École Militaire*, was founded in Paris in 1751, established through the efforts of the Marquise de Pompadour and the educator Paris-Duvernay In its early years the school was actually at Vincennes, and by 1753 there were 80 cadets. The new and superb building of the *École Militaire* was eventually inaugurated by Louis XV in 1760 with some 500 gentleman-cadets attending. It can still be seen at the opposite end of the Champ de Mars from the Eifel Tower. The school was specifically intended for the sons of noble families of modest means to enable them to obtain military training and a commission, if they passed the examinations, at royal or government expense. This partly met the continuing demand of the nobility for exclusive entitlement to an officer's commission and also the general need for well trained and adequately schooled officers. The curriculum included classes in French, German, mathematics, history, religion, drawing, geometry, geography, topography, tactics, military laws and army regulations. Physical activity included training in fencing, horse-riding and drill. Dancing and gentlemanly manners rounded out the education of the cadets. Latin and Italian, initially taught, were discontinued in 1769. The quality of education of the cadets arriving at the Military School varied greatly and, in 1764, a preparatory military school was opened at La Fleche, Normandy, to bring the less educated youths to an acceptable standard.

The benefits of military schooling could not actually be seen in the officer corps until after the Seven Years War (1756-1763), which was disastrous for France. The defeats of this war had spurred major reforms in the French army, including the abolition of the purchase system for commissions. As the years went by, more and more school-trained cadets were commissioned and some rose in the ranks. The modernization of the army went on and, in 1776, the military education system itself was reformed. On 1 February the Paris Military School, as it had existed until then, was abolished. In its stead a network of ten regional royal military schools was created. They were installed in abbeys and under the supervision of religious orders, with the classes given by civil, military and religious instructors. The objective was to provide both the army and the civil service with a cadre of thoroughly-trained officers. The schools were at Beaumont-en-Auge, Brienne, Effiat, Pont-á-Mousson, Pontlevoy, Rebais, Soreze, Thiron, Tournon and Vendome. Following the progressive ideas of the time, the curriculum was revised with more emphasis given to physical education, but the academic side was certainly not neglected. The students were taught French, Latin, German, history, geography, mathematics, drawing, moral and logic. They were admitted as young as eight years of age and would attend for up to six years. It was intended to have 50 to 60 military students to which were added an equal number of non-military boarding pupils. But these numbers were regularly exceeded. Brienne was supposed to have 120 students but in fact crowded in about 150.

The *École Militaire* at Paris was transformed into an institution of higher military learning and reopened on 17 July 1777 as the school of Gentlemen-Cadets. Its student numbers were now reduced to 100 but it was still housed in the buildings on the Champs de Mars. The school was divided into seven classes, one of which was for artillery and marine cadets. Entrants were selected by national examinations written by the senior students aged between 14 and 16 in the ten other schools. The élite who were accepted would have a couple more years of higher education with the prestigious status of Gentlemen-Cadet. Graduates were then commissioned in the better corps of the army or, occasionally, in the navy. Graduates from the other schools were incorporated into regiments as Gentlemen-Cadets. Such was the officer training in France at the time that the American Revolutionary War was breaking out.

The Uniforms of Military Schools

The uniform of the military cadets, including those at Brienne, from 1776 was a dark blue coat with scarlet collar, cuffs and lapels, white turnbacks with red fleur-de-lis, white metal buttons, dark blue waistcoat and breeches and stockings, black buckled shoes, plain hat. They could also wear black breeches, and white waistcoat and breeches appear to have been worn in the summer. There was also an undress dark blue 'surtout' coat with red collar and red fleur-de-lis on the turnbacks. The uniform of the Paris Military School (shown right) was a dark blue coat with scarlet collar, cuffs and lapels, white turnbacks, white metal buttons, scarlet waistcoat and breeches in winter, white waistcoat in summer, hat laced with silver.

notable example of this in the winter of 1783 when there was heavy snow. Napoleon organized the construction of snow redoubts according to Marshal Vauban's textbook plans and would be found leading the defence or the attack, always in the middle of a hail of snowballs and much shouting and cheering. The Brienne fathers did not disapprove.

TO THE PARIS MILITARY SCHOOL

As time passed, young Napoleon, whose name had now been gallicised to Bonaparte by removing the Italian 'u', was recognized as one of the brightest Brienne students. He was noticed by the Inspector General of Military Schools, the Chevalier de Keralio, who recommended him for higher military learning at *L'École Militaire*, in Paris, one of only two students from Brienne, the other being a M. de Castre. The Fathers wanted to keep him longer to improve his Latin but De Keralio overruled them, saying he had 'seen a spark in him' which must be further cultivated. In 1783, De Keralio wrote to Marshal Ségur that Bonaparte had excellent qualities, would make a

Gentleman-Cadet Napoleon Bonaparte in Paris sitting with his sister Elisa in the garden of the Saint-Cyr School in the fall of 1784. Saint-Cyr was a royal school for noble girls from families of modest means where Elisa had been admitted. Alone in Paris and very far from home, the brother and sister saw each other as much as they could. He was then fifteen, she was seven. (Print after JOB)

'good sailor' and should be promoted to the Paris school. De Keralio died soon after and the naval option proved too costly for the impoverished Bonaparte, so he turned to artillery as his speciality and, after a second successful examination, was sent to *L'École Militaire* in late 1784, a

year ahead of the usual six year schedule.

In the Paris school, living conditions were much more pleasant than in Brienne. The food was better, the Gentleman-Cadets were treated as the élite that they were, and they were right in the centre of Paris, which

Gentleman-Cadet Bonaparte at the Paris Military School, summer of 1785. (Print after A. Castaigne)

beckoned to be discovered. Even the Champs de Mars, right in front of the school, had its excitements in 1784. That summer the Montgolfier brothers made their hot air balloon flights and there was later a tale that Bonaparte tried to get on board one day, but it was actually another Gentleman-Cadet, Dupont de Charbon. Bonaparte would often visit his young sister Elisa, who was at the nearby Saint-Cyr school for noble girls. As a student in Paris, he was said to have forgotten there what little Latin he knew and proved so useless in German that Professor Bauer considered him to be almost an animal! But others thought differently. His writtten work may still have been shaky but his teacher, Professor Damiron considered his rough but passionate style to be 'like granite heated by a volcano'. His history teacher, M. Dumairon, saw farther than most when assessing Napoleon. He felt he would 'go far if circumstances favoured him.' His intelligence and concentration were mainly applied to the practical subjects and he became extraordinarily versed in the science of fortification. He preferred history to philosophy and excelled in mathematics. His defiant character led him to write a critical essay addressed to the Minister of War on the military education system and how to reform it!

At that time however, Bonaparte suffered a setback. Carlo di Buonaparte died in Montpellier, France, a devoted father but penniless and in debt. The rest of the family was left in Corsica in very humble circumstances. Napoleon's career prospects were about the only positive development. His brother Joseph was an amiable lad but not a leader, so Napoleon, in spite of the distance, became the main support to his mother and wrote her many letters. There was no time to lose and he had to obtain a commission as soon as possible. He passed the examinations to become a subaltern officer and, on 1 September 1785, he was commissioned as a second lieutenant in the La Fere Regiment of the Royal Corps of Artillery. He had spent less than a year at the Paris Military School but was as fully educated as he could be in the science and art of ordnance. His student days were over.

To be continued in the next issue.

SELECT BIBLIOGRAPHY

Arnaud, M. A., and C. L. F. Panckouke, *Memoir of the Public and Private Life of Napoleon Bonaparte*, (Boston, 1841)

Aubry, Octave, *Napoléon*, (Paris, 1936)

Norvins, M. de, *Histoire de Napoléon*, (Paris, 1868)

Sloane, William M., 'Life of Napoleon Bonaparte', *The Century Magazine*, (November 1894)

Lienhart, Dr., and René Humbert, *Les Uniformes de l'Armée française*, Vol. IV, (Liepzig, 1902)

ABOUT THE AUTHOR

René Chartrand is a military historian and film consultant. He has written many books with Osprey, and after researching in Britain and Portugal, is currently finishing three Men-at-Arms volumes on the Portuguese Army of the Napoleonic Wars.

Flodden Field, 1513. Flushed by the initial success of their assault on the English right flank, Highland and Lowland Scots, intent on taking Sir Edmund Howard for ransom, are thwarted by the timely intervention of a troop of Border horse led by the Bastard Heron. (© Copyright Osprey Publishing from Men-at-Arms 279 The Border Reivers by Keith Durham, artwork by Angus McBride)

Flodden Field 1513
Scotland's Bloodiest Day

BY JOHN BARRATT

THE COMING OF WAR

On 9 September 1513, 34-year-old King James IV of Scotland, the last British monarch to die in battle, met his end at Flodden in one of the bloodiest encounters in the long centuries of conflict between England and her northern neighbour.

The origins of the battle lay in the ambitions of King Henry VIII. Newly established on the English throne, the young monarch was anxious to enhance his prestige and gain military glory at the expense of England's traditional foe, France. Having joined the Holy League against King Louis, on 30 June 1513

Henry set sail for England's continental outpost of Calais at the head of a splendidly equipped army of some 24,000 men to join forces with the Emperor Maximillian in an invasion of France.

But Henry's action triggered hostilities nearer home. King James IV

The Scottish Army

The Scots lacked regular soldiers in government service and the bulk of the Scottish army was raised either from the retinues of the nobility and gentry or by levy. As the relationship between the monarch and his magnates was less regulated and secure than in England, more use was made of the levy, in which the entire male population between 16 and 60 was theoretically liable for service. Each magnate, bourgh or county would be set a quota of men which it was expected to provide. As in England, those selected to serve would normally be expected to provide at least part of their own equipment, and serve at their own or their local communities' expense for 40 days. After this time the cost was to be sustained by the government, making prolonged campaigning problematic. Training and weapon inspection, were supposed to be carried out at regular musters or 'wappenshaws'. Motivation was often low, and desertion high, though enthusiasm in 1513 seems, initially at least, to have been somewhat greater. Nobility and gentry normally wore at least some plate armour, whilst the mass of the Lowlands levy had 'jacks', and sallet helmets, and in some cases a light shield or 'pavise'. Highlanders tended to wear little or no armour, and were commonly armed with bows, broadswords and various types of 'lochaber' axes.

At Flodden, with the possible exception of some of Home's Borderers and the Highland contingent, much of the Scots army was armed with pikes. The French are known to have supplied James with at least 6,000 pikes and a similar number of 'spears' (possibly halberds) though a report that only about 2,000 pikes were captured at Flodden may indicate that the Scots were not as universally equipped with this weapon as sometimes suggested.

The Scots defeat is sometimes ascribed to lack of familarity with pike tactics. Although the bulk of the levies had probably rarely manouvred together in large formations, there is evidence that the long pike had been in use in Scotland since about 1474, when the Scots Parliament passed an Act, (repeated in 1481) decreeing that no imported spears, nor any manufactured in Scotland, should be less than 6 'ells' (18 feet 6 inches) in length.

James took particular pride in his train of artillery, which in the Flodden campaign consisted of 17 guns of various sizes, commanded by Robert Borthwick, appointed as Master Gunner by King James in 1511. Though the Scots siege guns proved highly effective in the opening stages of the campaign, the lighter pieces seem to have had little effect at Flodden.

of Scotland, though he had attempted for several months to avert the looming conflict, was pledged to support his country's long standing French ally. Whilst hoping for peace, the Scottish monarch had also been preparing for war. English suspicions of Scottish intentions were heightened by evidence that James had been purchasing pikes, armour and gunpowder from the Low Countries, and that French military 'advisers' had been despatched to train the Scots in Continental tactics, particularly the use of the pike. On 22 May a formal military alliance was signed between France and Scotland. The stage was set for a major trial between the pike-armed phalanx, employed with great success by practitioners such as the Swiss, and the traditional English arms of longbow and bill.

Before leaving for France, the King had entrusted the defence of his English realm to 70-year-old Thomas Howard, Earl of Surrey, with the warning: 'My lord, I trust not the Scots, therefore I pray you be not negligent.' The advice was hardly needed, for there was no more experienced a soldier in England than the Earl of Surrey. His military career extended back to the Wars of the Roses, when he had fought at Bosworth for Richard III against King Henry's father. Despite his old allegiance, Surrey became one of the most trusted servants of the new Tudor dynasty, and, though age and infirmity now forced the arrogant, tough old soldier to travel by carriage instead of on horseback, his vast experience and noted guile would render him a formidable opponent.

Surrey and the English Council of State, headed by Queen Katherine, were at first uncertain of enemy intentions. The Scots might limit themselves to border raids, but it quickly became clear that James had a more ambitious strategy. Noted for his

chivalry, and his relatively liberal outlook, the Scottish King was determined to honour his alliance with King Louis, and had already promised that if Henry invaded France he would take such actions as would 'make him glad to return.'

Despite extravagant claims made for propaganda purposes by James, and repeated by some later writers, Scottish military aims in 1513 were strictly limited. Now equipped with a powerful artillery train, James planned to repeat his earlier strategy: besiege and capture Norham and other English border garrisons, and, if all went well, bring Surrey to battle in an advantageous situation and inflict on him a reverse that would divert English efforts from France. Believing England's best troops to be on the Continent, James might never have a better opportunity to demonstrate his military prowess.

Thomas Howard, Earl of Surrey. (By courtesy of the Trustees of the British Museum)

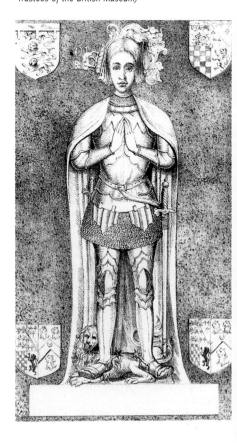

English infantry at Flodden. From left to right, a billman: an archer from Sir Edward Stanley's contingent and a man-at-arms from the Earl of Surrey's Division. (© Copyright Osprey Publishing from Men-at-Arms 191 Henry VIII's Army by Paul Cornish, artwork by Angus McBride)

The English Army

The English standing army consisted of no more than a few hundred men in the royal household and the garrisons of Berwick and Calais, none of whom were present at Flodden. In time of war some of the English forces came from contingents provided from the households of certain leading magnates and gentry. However the bulk of the troops were provided by the county militias, in which all men aged 16-60 were liable for service, with command usually exercised by the local gentry. Training varied, theoretically taking place at periodic musters, with militia from areas under more immediate threat, such as the Northern Border counties and the South coast, being generally of a higher standard. It was also common practice to engage foreign professionals and mercenaries, although none seem to have served at Flodden. The basic tactical unit was a company of about 100 men.

English tactics involved the combination of longbow and pole-type weapons which had been the mainstay of their armies for almost a century. Although there is some evidence that the quality of the English longbowman had declined from its peak of a century earlier, he still had the edge over the hand-held firearms generally available, none of which seem to have been employed by the English forces at Flodden. However, plate armour, of the type worn by the Scottish nobility and gentry, was increasingly resistant to arrows, and the archers at Flodden were perhaps more of an irritant than a battle-winning weapon.

Mainstay of the English forces was the billman, armed with a pole-type weapon, most commonly the 6-8 foot long 'English' bill, which could be highly effective at close quarters, though its user required considerably more training than sometimes suggested. Most infantry were equipped with sallet-type helmet, and a quilted 'jack' or the type of back and breast plate generally known as 'Almain rivet'.

The only cavalry present were some Border horse, contingents of which fought on both sides. Usually under their own local leaders, and armed with an 8-foot 'border' lance, sword, and most commonly protected by sallet helmet and quilted jacket, the Borderer could prove a very effective light cavalryman, although their lack of discipline, low commitment, and tendency to loot and plunder indiscriminately, made them very unreliable allies.

Like his Scottish rival, King Henry was keenly interested in artillery, and a considerable number of guns were imported from the Continent. Surrey had a number of light pieces at Flodden, though they seem to have been little more effective than their Scots counterparts.

An earlier action at Millfield had confirmed Surrey's feeling that major hostilities with Scotland were imminent. Heading north to Pontefract with his own small force of household troops, the Earl summoned a Council of War of the leading gentry of the North of England, and issued orders for them to be prepared to muster their tenants at one hour's notice, with a relay of post horses in readiness to carry news to London and the further parts of England.

Rather than mustering his forces prematurely, with the risk that he would be forced to disband through lack of supplies before Scottish intentions became clear, Surrey instead instructed the Constable of Norham to be ready to fight a delaying action, and continued to sift the conflicting reports which reached him from Scotland. Though rumour credited the Scots army mustering on Borough Moor near Edinburgh with 100,000 men, its actual strength of 30–40,000 troops, coupled with its train of artillery and the leavening of experience provided by the French contingent under the Compte d'Aussi and numbering 50 men at arms and 40 captains, which was formidable enough.

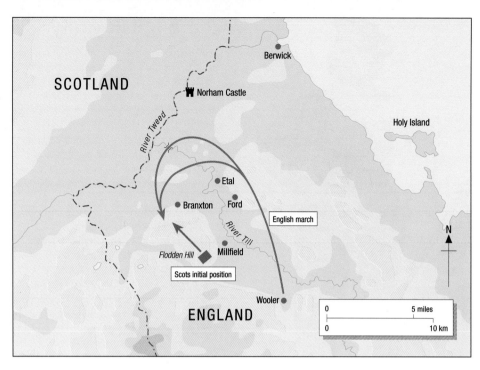

The approach to Flodden. (© Copyright Osprey Publishing)

THE CAMPAIGN

On 22 August the Scottish invasion began, with considerable initial success. Wark Castle fell after two days, and the Scots moved against Norham. Despite its commander's boasts that he would hold out until Henry had returned from France, Norham, battered by Scottish guns and hit by successive waves of assaulting troops, surrendered on 29 August, and on 3 September nearby Etal Castle succumbed after a brief bombardment.

News of the Scottish invasion reached Surrey at Pontefract on 25 August, and: 'in the foulest night and day there could be,' he hastened north via York, Durham and Newcastle, picking up reinforcements and the moral support of the fabled Banner of St Cuthbert from Durham Cathedral, and arrived at Alnwick on 3 September. Here Surrey rendezvoused with contingents of levies from all parts of the North of England. Most welcome was a contingent from the English fleet, consisting of about 928

men-at-arms and 300 archers, led by his son, the Lord Admiral, Thomas Howard. A small dark man, 'wyse, hardy and of great credence and experience', Howard had gained a notable reputation in operations against the French coast, and probably played a key role in events of the coming days. Besides Howard's contingent, Surrey mustered some 11,500 men, mostly mounted billmen and archers, with a few demi-lances. Also coming in as reinforcements were 6,500 similarly equipped troops from Lancashire and Cheshire under Sir Edward Stanley, giving Surrey in all about 20,000 men.

Before setting out from Alnwick to confront the invader, Surrey re-organised his army. It was formed into two main divisions, or 'battles', each supported by two smaller formations known as 'wings'. The exact strength of each division is unknown, but the 'vaward' under the Admiral seems to have been the strongest, with perhaps 7,000 men, whilst Surrey's 'battle' may have totalled up to 5,000.

As Surrey may have learnt from intelligence sources, King James was by now facing problems. His levies had expected to serve for no more than forty days, and, supporting the idea that only a short campaign had been planned, the contracts of the professional gunners manning the Scottish artillery would shortly expire. Many of the King's senior commanders felt that they had now fulfilled their obligations to the French, and favoured returning home, and this opinion was expressed in more practical form by an unknown, but evidently significant, number of their men who deserted. And although supplies were for the moment adequate, maintaining the army in the field would soon become a problem.

On Monday 5 September, Surrey began a cautious advance towards Bolton, about eight miles from the current Scots position. At the same time he sent King James a formal challenge to battle on the following Friday, which was apparently accepted. However the Scots King, whatever chivalric statements he made for public consumption, perhaps hearkening to his French advisers, had no intention of fighting at a disadvantage. Surrey discovered on 7 September that the Scots army was drawn up in a strong defensive position on Flodden Hill, protected by marshy ground which would crowd any English attack onto a narrow frontage overlooked by the Scots guns.

APPROACH TO BATTLE

Early on 8 September, in continuing foul weather, the entire English army marched some eight miles directly north to Barmoor Wood, which lay to the east of Flodden Hill. Next day, probably at Thomas Howard's suggestion, it was decided to cross the River Till and swing westwards in

OSPREY MILITARY JOURNAL

ENLIST TODAY!

THE INTERNATIONAL REVIEW OF MILITARY HISTORY

From the world's leading publisher of illustrated military history
(more than 500 authoritative titles in print)

•

Fascinating articles on military history – battles, campaigns, great commanders, tactics
and strategies – around the world, from ancient times to the present day

•

Expert guidance for the enthusiast: modeling, gaming, collecting, re-enacting,
travelling, reading, viewing. Plus an international calendar of events, and historic sites to visit

•

Fully illustrated in Osprey's unique style with artwork, maps, charts, tables and photographs

•

Bi-monthly (six issues per year), 64 pages per issue

BECOME A CHARTER SUBSCRIBER TODAY USING THIS FORM AND BE SURE OF RECEIVING EACH ISSUE ON PUBLICATION

 **YES!** I would like to subscribe to *Osprey Military Journal* for one year (six issues)

PLEASE MAIL/FAX THIS FORM TO THE APPROPRIATE ADDRESS BELOW, OR CONTACT US BY TELEPHONE OR E-MAIL

USA/Canada (N. America)	**US$39.95**	**Europe**	**£33.50**
UK	**£25.50**	**Rest of World**	**£42.50**

(all prices periodicals postage paid)

Mr/Mrs/Ms   Name: First .... Last ....

Address ....

....

Zip / postcode .... Country ....Telephone no...............................

USA / CANADA

Osprey Direct USA
P.O. Box 130
Sterling Hts MI 48311-0130
USA

Tel: 810 795 2763
Fax: 810 795 4266
E-mail: info@ospreydirectusa.com

GIVE a gift subscription to someone who will enjoy *Osprey Military Journal*

Please send a one year subscription to: (PLEASE INDICATE ANY ADDITIONAL ADDRESSES ON A SEPARATE SHEET)

Mr/Mrs/Ms   Name: First .... Last ....

Address ....

....

Zip / postcode .... Country ....Telephone no...............................

UK / EUROPE / REST OF WORLD

Osprey Direct UK
P.O. Box 140
Wellingborough
Northants NN8 4ZA
UK

Tel: +44 (0)1933 443863
Fax: +44 (0)1933 443849
E-mail: info@ospreydirect.co.uk

Qty	Price		Total
....	US$39.95 (addresses in N. America)	US$	....
....	£25.50 (addresses in UK)	£	....
....	£33.50 (addresses elsewhere in Europe)	£	....
....	£42.50 (addresses in Rest of World)	£	....

TOTAL AMOUNT TO PAY   US$ / £ ....

If Osprey Military Journal does not meet your expectations, cancel your subscription and receive a refund for remaining issues.

☐ Please charge my credit card   ☐ Visa   ☐ MasterCard

Card number ☐☐☐☐ ☐☐☐☐ ☐☐☐☐ ☐☐☐☐   Expiry ☐☐ ☐☐

☐ Payment enclosed (cheques payable to Osprey Publishing)

☐ Please tick if you do not wish to receive information on selected goods or services which may be of interest to you

Signature ....

Please quote source code **MJ2.4**

PLEASE INDICATE WHEN YOU WOULD LIKE TO START YOUR SUBSCRIPTION: NEXT ISSUE (2.5 – out September 2000) ☐   OTHER, PLEASE SPECIFY ....

Erhard Schoon The Siege of Munster, c. 1536, early-16th-century demi-culverins in siege operations. Similar artillery pieces were used by James IV at Norham Castle.

order to threaten the Scots position from the rear. It was a high-risk strategy, which left the road into England open to James, and Surrey possibly trapped with his back to the River Tweed. Nevertheless, it also placed the English squarely between the Scots and home, and Surrey and his commanders probably calculated that this would be unacceptable to James' levies.

As the English mounted columns, headed by the Admiral's division, crossed the River Till at Milford and Twizel Bridge, they were dangerously vulnerable to a flank attack, but the Scots, although the first stages of the enemy movement must have been partially visible from Flodden Hill, remained inactive. It may be that they were uncertain of Surrey's intentions, believing him to be heading for Berwick in order to re-supply. Equally

Battle of Fornovo 1495 – a Swiss pike block showing how only the leading ranks could effectively engage the enemy. Note the light artillery accompanying the column.

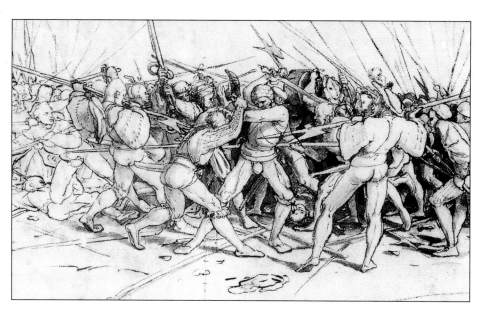

Holbein the Younger Infantry Battle, c. 1530. The hand-to-hand fighting at Flodden must have resembled the scene depicted here. (Kunstmuseum, Basle)

possibly, divisions in the Scots Council of War, which were a feature of the campaign, again surfaced, paralysing decision-making at a critical moment. By mid-morning, however, it had become apparent that the English objective was 300-foot-high Branxton Hill, about a mile north of Flodden Hill, where they would block the Scots line of retreat and force them to assault a formidable defensive position.

James ordered his men to about-face and occupy Branxton Hill first. With the movements of both sides partially obscured by smoke from burning refuse in their abandoned camp, the Scots army, marching in five colums, four roughly in line abreast and one in reserve, headed north, and reached the crest of Branxton Hill ahead of their opponents.

It would still have been possible for James to have reverted to his defensive strategy, and again await an English attack in a position of advantage, and he has frequently been criticised for ensuing events.

However, the prospect which greeted the leading Scots troops as they crested Branxton Hill at about 2pm seemed ripe with opportunity. The English army had become considerably strung out in crossing the River Till, with the result that the Admiral's division was perhaps a mile and a half ahead of the rest, and further disordered by crossing boggy ground in the valley of the Pallin Burn. If James moved quickly enough, he might be able to destroy his opponents piecemeal.

Approaching Branxton Church, Thomas Howard sighted enemy columns massing on Branxton Hill, and sent a desperate message to his father, urging haste. At the same time he halted his own advance at the foot of the hill. As Surrey's division came up it gradually deployed on Howard's left, but for almost two hours the English remained dangerously vulnerable to attack.

James proved unable to grasp the opportunity. The massive Scottish columns were both slow-moving and difficult to deploy. By the time that James had brought up the bulk of his troops, at about 4pm, the English were prepared to receive them.

THE ARMIES ARRAYED

The Scots, by this time possibly totalling about 30,000 men, were deployed on the crest of Branxton Hill, with four columns forward, about 200 yards apart, and some of their lighter guns probably stationed in the intervals. On the left was the division, perhaps 3,000 strong, commanded by the Earls of Home and Huntley, consisting of Borderers, some of whom had been involved in the defeat at Millfield, and levies from the Aberdeen area. Next came the larger column led by the Earls of Crawford and Montrose, consisting of up to 5,000 levies from Perth, Forfar and Fife. King James himself, marching under his banner of St Andrew, commanded probably the largest division, formed from the men of Stirling, Linlithgow and the Lothians. As with the divisions to his left, James and his nobles and gentry, in their full plate armour, formed the first rank of the column, with the more lightly equipped levies in up to 20 ranks to their rear. On the right of the Scottish line was the division led by the Earl of Argyll. Consisting mainly of Highlanders, more lightly equipped than the remainder of the army, this was the least effective of the Scots divisions.

Some distance to the rear, and perhaps still moving up, was a fifth column, of about 1,500 men, under the Earl of Bothwell, consisting of his own and some Lothian men, together with the French men-at-arms.

The English army was deployed about 600 yards away, along a lower ridge which ran parallel to Branxton Hill, just to the south of Branxton village. Surrey had amended his original organisation so that his army now formed four divisions corresponding to those of the Scots, with a small reserve of Border horse. On the right was the division which had originally been one of the wings of the 'vaward', but now consisting of about 3,000 mainly Lancashire and Cheshire levies under Sir Edmund Howard, Surrey's younger son. To its left, perhaps 7,000 strong, was the division led by Thomas Howard, the Lord Admiral, consisting of his men from the fleet and the Durham levies. Next, with about 5,000 men, was Surrey's own division, now termed the 'rearward'. As well as Surrey's household troops it included about 3,000 Yorkshire troops, with a small Lancashire contingent under Sir John Stanley. On Surrey's flank the English main line was completed by Sir Edward Stanley's division of about 3,000 Lancashire and Cheshire men. Surrey's artillery was positioned in the intervals of his divisions. The reserve, of about 2,000 Borderers under Lord Dacre, may have included both mounted and dismounted troops. They were of decidedly mixed quality, a number having already slipped off to steal the horses that the dismounted English army had left in the rear.

THE BATTLE BEGINS

Proceedings opened with an generally ineffective exchange of artillery fire. It has been suggested that the English cannon fire stung the Scots into launching a piecemeal assault, but it

seems more likely that James had always intended a general attack, to be delivered, according to accepted Continental tactics, by the columns in echelon, starting from the left, but which rapidly became disorganised. James himself was condemned both at the time and later, for his decision to place himself in the front rank of one of the attacking columns. In 1497 the French ambassador had noted of the King: 'He is courageous, even more than a king should be. I have seen him often undertake the most dangerous things … he is not a good captain, because he begins to fight before he has given his orders. He said to me that his subjects serve him with their persons and goods, in just and unjust quarrel, exactly as he likes, and that therefore he does not think it right to begin any warlike undertaking without being the first in danger.' It was, of course, still the expected role of a monarch to demonstrate active leadership in battle, and it was claimed by Tudor propagandists that Henry VIII had to be dissuaded by his councillors from similar involvement

at the battle of the Spurs. It is also unclear, once his initial dispositions had been made and fighting begun, what significant influence on the conduct of the battle James could have had if he had remained aloof from the fray.

The pike phalanx relied for its effectiveness on keeping its formation and the impetus of its assault. The Scots advance was certainly hindered by the slippery descent down Branxton Hill, followed by a 200 yard ascent to the English-held ridge, and to some extent by enemy archery and artillery fire, some of whose shots brought down eight or nine men at a time in the close-packed Scots ranks. But it seems likely that the effects have sometimes been exaggerated. The English guns cannot have fired many shots in the relatively short time it took the Scots to advance 600 yards, whilst the bowmen were hindered both by firing into a strong wind and by the damp conditions which had slackened their bow strings. Their fire also fell mainly on the well-armoured front ranks of the Scottish column.

Certainly the impetus of Home's Borderers was little affected. First to make contact, they fell on Edmund Howard's division. Many of Howard's men quickly broke under the onslaught, although Sir Edmund himself and some of his men fought on desperately around his standard, until rescued by an opportune countercharge by Lord Dacre and those of his Border horse that had not fled at the first sound of cannon fire. Howard and his survivors reformed on the flank of the Admiral's division, now locked in its own fierce contest.

Observers noted the discipline with which the two centre Scots columns, of Crawford and Montrose and King James, advanced: 'in good order, after the Almayn's manner, without speaking a word.' Few details are known of the engagement between

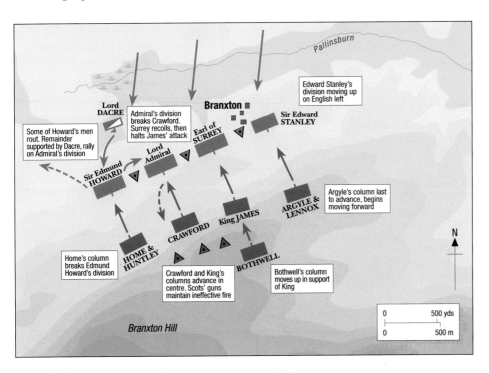

The battle of Flodden, the early stages. (© Copyright Osprey Publishing)

The 'Phalanx' Revived

The two predominant European infantry tactical systems of the period were the combination of longbow and man-at-arms, armed principally with bill or halberd, favoured by the English, and the pike and halberd equipped column, based on the phalanx of classical times, and normally presenting a square or rectangular formation, up to 24 ranks deep. With pikes up to 18 feet long, and its ranks densely massed, a pike column was virtually impervious to cavalry attack, and, if well handled, could rapidly dispose of opposing infantry, as demonstrated by the Swiss in their campaigns against Burgundy.

Yet the pike column, even if better-trained than the Scots at Flodden, was far from invincible. Its densely packed ranks were vulnerable to effective firepower, could be disrupted by unfavourable terrain, or flank attack, and, as shown in the defeat of the French pike columns at Cerignola (1503) and Ravenna (1512), could be countered by determined and well-trained infantry. In the latter engagement German landsknechts in French employ had failed to break the Spanish ranks with their charge, and became involved in close-quarter fighting with Spanish sword and buckler men, whose greater mobility and effectiveness in hand-to-hand combat proved decisive. It was a foretaste of Flodden which apparently passed unheeded in Scotland.

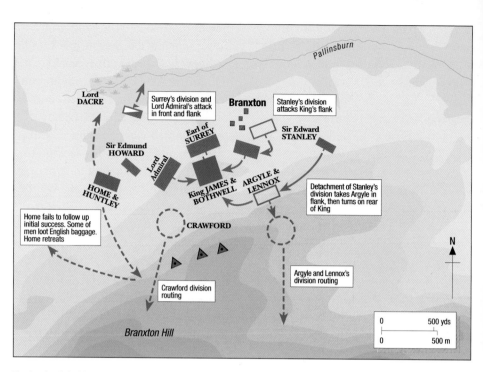

The battle of Flodden, the Scottish defeat. (© Copyright Osprey Publishing)

the Admiral and Crawford's column, except that, possibly aided by the uneven ground, and possible superiority of numbers, the English held their ground against the first shock of the attack, and a fierce struggle began, in which the Admiral ordered that no quarter be given.

Very shortly afterwards the King's column came into contact with Surrey's division, which recoiled under the impact for perhaps 300 yards. Then the English rallied and the Scots column came to a halt.

BLOODBATH

A new phase of the battle now began. If the initial assault of a phalanx failed to break its opponent, its long pikes were ineffective in close-quarter hand-to-hand fighting. 'Disappointed

of their long spears upon which they relied', the leading Scots ranks fell on with maces and swords. However, they quickly found themselves at a disadvantage against the more lightly armoured and mobile English billmen and halberdiers, who handled their weapons with a deadly skill the Scots proved unable to match. In savage combat, the slower moving plate-armoured men of the leading Scots ranks found themselves engaged individually by teams of two or three English billmen, working in close co-operation: 'who did beat and hew them down with some pain and danger to Englishmen, [for] these fellows [the Scots] were such large, strong men, that they would not fall when four or five bills struck them.' It was brutal bloody fighting, in which the packed Scots ranks proved at a disadvantage, for as the men of the first ranks fell dead or wounded or became exhausted, it was very difficult for the less well-armed men in the rear to move up to replace them.

The impetus of his assault lost, and Crawford's column possibly already

breaking, King James urgently needed support. As we have seen, Home's column had broken Edmund Howard's men, but the Borderers failed to follow up their success. Various reasons have been suggested for this, including Home's reputed refusal to move against the flank of the Admiral's division with the comment: 'He does best that does for himself', and rumours of a tacit deal done with Dacre's Borderers. Although Home was afterwards made a scapegoat for the Scots defeat, and accused of treachery, it is difficult to see what advantage he could thus have gained. It is more likely that, with a number of leaders casualties in the first engagement, he was unable to rally his loosely disciplined men in time to intervene before the outcome in the centre – Home's view of which was in any case largely hidden by the Piper's Hill ridge – had been decided.

Some at least of Bothwell's men managed to join up with the King's column, but James' men were in increasing difficulties as the Admiral's division, having broken Crawford's

Flodden by Burgkmair – the defeat of James' Division, the king lies dead in the foreground. Both terrain and the equipment of the combatants are inaccurate, the latter betraying a strong German influence. (British Library)

found just in front of Surrey's original position, he may have been struck down quite early in the battle. In any event, by the time dusk put an end to further fighting, with the effective destruction of the King's division, the English, though they were not fully aware of it until daylight, had won a resounding victory. Home's division, which had remained in the vicinity during the night, retreated at dawn, leaving Surrey's men to take possession of the abandoned Scots artillery.

AFTERMATH

As well as their King, the Scots had lost the flower of their nobility and up to 10,000 other dead. English losses were in the region of 1,500.

The bloodbath of Flodden did not end the conflict, as raid and counter-raid continued along the Anglo-Scots border, but the first great contest between pike, bow and bill had resulted in a decisive success for the latter weapons. More importantly for King Henry, with the threat from his northern neighbour effectively removed, he was free to pursue the chimera of military glory in France.

SUGGESTED READING

Burne, A. H, *Battlefields of England*, (London, 1951)

Cornish, Paul and McBride, Angus, Men at Arms 191: *Henry VIII's Army*, (Osprey Publishing, 1991)

Cruickshank, Charles, *Henry VIII and the Invasion of France*, (Stroud, 1990)

Durham, Keith and Mc Bride, Angus, Men at Arms 279: *Border Reivers*, (Osprey Publishing, 1995)

Elliot, Fitzwilliam, *The Battle of Flodden and the Raids of 1513*, (Tonbridge, 1991)

Mackay, Mackenzie W. *The Secret of Flodden*, (London 1931)

Miller, Douglas, Men at Arms 94: *The Swiss, 1300-1500*, (Osprey Publishing, 1976)

Miller, Douglas and Embleton, Gerry, Men at Arms 94: *The Swiss, 1300-1500* (Osprey Publishing, 1979)

Oman, Charles, *A History of War in the Sixteenth Century*, (London, 1987)

Phillips, Gervase, *The Anglo-Scots Wars 1513-1550*, (Woodbridge, 1999)

ABOUT THE AUTHOR

John Barratt has a lifelong interest in military history, especially of the 16th and 17th centuries, and has contributed articles to a number of journals. He is also the author of *Cavaliers: the Royalist Army at War* to be published by Sutton in 2000.

column, began to turn against their left flank. Worse was about to follow.

On the far Scot's right the advance of Argyll's column, intended to be the last to hit the enemy, seems to have been particularly disrupted and slowed by the uneven ground. This was fortunate for the English, as the opposing division of Sir Edward Stanley was the last to form up. Argyll does not actually seem to have made contact with Stanley's main force, whose archery may have had more effect on the lightly armoured Highlanders than was the case elsewhere, and may have been preparing to move in support of the King when he was hit by a flank attack by part of Stanley's division concealed by the uneven ground. Already wavering after the loss of several of their chieftains to enemy fire, the

Highlanders broke and fled, and Stanley was free to turn against the right flank and rear of James' column.

Isolated and under attack from all sides, the fate of the King's column was sealed. James' men died hard. Gradually pushed back into a clump around the Standard of St Andrew they fought on grimly. An English writer agreed that the Scots: 'fought manly, and were determined either to win the field or to die, they were also as well appointed as was possible at all points with arms and harness, so that few of them were slain with arrows, how be it the bills did beat and hew them down with some pain and danger to Englishmen.'

It is not clear when King James fell. As the body later rather uncertainly identified as his, with an arrow wound to the face and several bill injuries, was

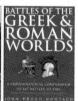

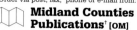

Night and the Hill!

Greene's Thin Blue Line at Gettysburg

CARL SMITH

For the Union, 1 July 1863 had been a bad day. General Robert E. Lee's Confederates had shoved the Army of the Potomac east and south from McPherson's Ridge and Oak Ridge out of Gettysburg and back to their 'fishhook' position on the high ground formed by the Round Tops, Cemetery Ridge and Hill, and Culp's Hill. The Union troops had been driven through the town, only just making it to the lower slopes of Cemetery Hill, where they had rallied and reformed as sundown approached. Lee, who regretted that: 'we did not or we could not pursue our advantage', was still uncertain of the Union's dispositions the following morning so an early attack was out of the question. However, he was not intending to stay on the defensive, as he clearly stated early on 2 July: 'The enemy is here and if we do not whip him, he will whip us'.

The Confederates already knew the value of a strong defensive position from their experience at Fredericksburg. To carry one by assault, it was generally accepted that the attacker needed minimum odds of three to one in favour. At Gettysburg the Confederates were to learn that assaults against such positions were doomed at these odds. Pickett's charge

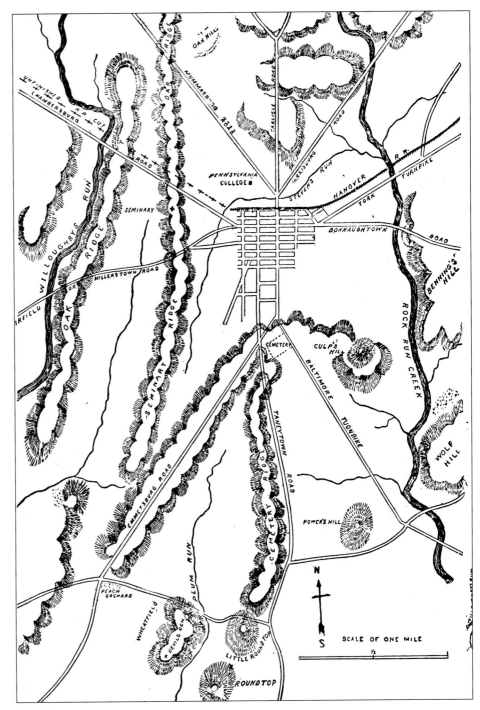

Contemporary map showing Culp's Hill in relation to the town of Gettysburg. Culp's Hill formed the tip of the Union fishhook defense and protected the important Baltimore Pike.

up Cemetery Ridge is the best-known Confederate failure, but there were also attacks on 2 and 3 July that could have decided the battle: on Little Round Top with its hastily assembled defense, and on Culp's Hill. Here the Confederates arguably came as close to success as at any other point in the battle.

THE UNION POSITION

Culp's Hill rises 140 feet above Gettysburg at its northern peak to the west of Cemetery Hill. Between the two hills the Baltimore Pike runs southeast from the town; for the Army of the Potomac this was a critical line of communication. Northeast is Benner's Hill and the Hanover Road out to the east. Rock Creek runs between Culp's Hill and Benner's Hill and, turning south, separates the former from Wolf's Hill to the east. Although passable in many places, Rock Creek was not easy to ford in this area and is referred to as a ravine in some contemporary accounts. The lower ground to the east and southeast was marshy swamp on either side of Spangler's Spring. Culp's Hill's northern and eastern slopes are liberally strewn with rocks and boulders with cliff-like outcrops rising 15-20 feet in places and deeply shadowed by thick and closely spaced trees. Here it is naturally defended and a place made for ambushes. The southern and western slopes, inside the Union position, are more gentle.

For most of 2 July XII Corps was positioned on the crest of Culp's Hill, nearly 10,000 men under the command of General Alpheus S. Williams, holding the right of the Union line, the barbed tip of the fishhook. Captain Lewis R. Stegman wrote of his regiment: 'The One hundred and second New York was formed in line upon the side of a precipitous hill … Skirmishers and pickets from First Corps occupied our front, but were relieved by detail. The men were ordered to build breastworks, and did so with the best material at hand, cord wood and rock, making, however, a strong line.' Captain Joseph Moore of the 147th Pennsylvania wrote '… the pioneer corps was not at hand, and bayonets, tin pans, tin cups etc. were improvised as implements in the construction of earthworks.' Traces of their overnight efforts can still be seen today. Combining man-made protection with natural features and commanding enfilading and intersecting fields of fire, the Union position was a good one.

At Culp's Hill, more than half a mile of trenches was held by men from I Corps' 1st Division and XII Corps. Dawn was slightly after 4.30am, and

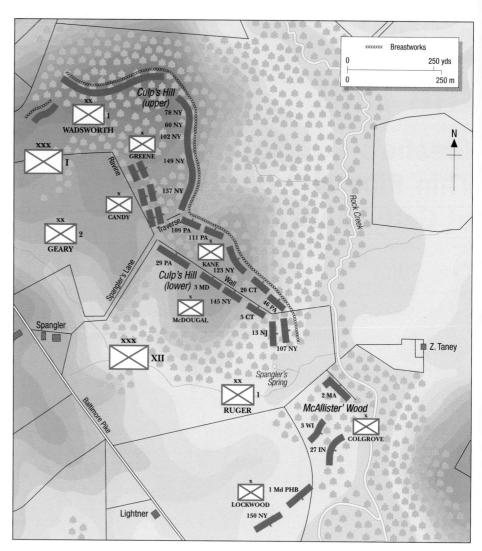

The Union position for most of 2 July. The marshy ground on either side of Spangler's Spring secured the apparent gap between the main line and McAllister Woods. The Confederates were beyond Rock Creek to the east and north. Both sides had pickets well forward in the valley.

The woods on the north and eastern slopes of Culp's Hill were dark, thick with aged trees. Shadows and underbrush obscured vision. It was a place made for ambush. Union skirmishers' hit and run tactics slowed up the Confederate advance.

A contemporary lithograph from Harper's Weekly depicts the rough breastworks composed of stones, earth and fallen logs that Greene's brigade used to defend Culp's Hill. Although in some disrepair presently, these breastworks stood for several decades after the battle.

within an hour the temperature was in the high seventies and climbing. Through the wooded slopes to the east, hot thirsty Union soldiers could catch glimpses of Rock Creek below them. Only skirmishers were close enough to drink from it, but Confederate pickets and skirmishers made it unsafe to venture to the water's edge. Until now this had been a campaign of speedy movement; through most of 2 July it was a waiting war for the men in blue and gray.

THE CONFEDERATE PLAN

By late morning of 2 July Lee had decided on a three-pronged attack. The main thrust was to be directed across the Emmitsburg Road towards Cemetery Ridge There was also to be a flanking attack on the Union left, which was not then thought to extend as far south as was actually the case, and a simultaneous diversionary move against the Union right, curling around Culp's Hill. This feint was designed to pin down forces that might otherwise strengthen the lines

facing north and west from Cemetery Hill and Cemetery Ridge. Lieutenant-General Richard Ewell in charge of II Corps had orders to escalate to a full attack if the opportunity arose.

Because of delays in assembling the forces for Lieutenant-General James Longstreet's main thrust from the west, and then some cumbersome manoeuvring, the real fighting did not begin until about 4.30pm.

PRELIMINARIES

All day long intermittent rifle fire had crackled along the front between the skirmishers on either side of Rock Creek. From around the time of Longstreet's attack some artillery fire had been exchanged, with the Union gunners finally winning the duel. Lieutenant Edward D. Muhlenberg of the 4th US Artillery, commanding XII Corps artillery wrote: 'The enemy seriously annoying the left of the line of the Twelfth, a vacant space eligible for a battery was found about 200 yards on the right of I Corps. At 3.30pm one gun (10-pounder Parrott),

George S Greene was borne in 1801 making him one of the oldest men to fight at Gettysburg. He was a West Point graduate, commissioned in the artillery, and served 13 years, mainly as an instructor. He left the army to pursue a successful career as a civil engineer. He joined the Union army in January 1862 as colonel of the 60th New York and was given a brigade that April. He saw a lot of action before Gettysburg, in the Shenandoah Valley, at Cedar Mountain, at Antietam, where he commanded a division, and at Chancellorsville.

The construction of field fortifications was not general practice but Greene had used breastworks once before, at Chancellorsville. There is a record of some debate in which General Geary opposed the digging of trenches on Culp's Hill on grounds that they reduced men's fighting effectiveness. Greene, known as a firm but just disciplinarian, successfully argued that the saving of men's lives was more important and his expertise as an artilleryman and engineer would have been valuable in the design of the works. The quite elaborate fortifications constructed overnight and through 2 July were a critical factor in the battle, as was Greene's outstanding leadership. After Gettysburg Greene went to Tennessee with XII Corps and was wounded in October 1863 only recovering in time for Sherman's march to the sea. In peacetime he resumed his career becoming president of the American Society of Civil Engineers. He died in 1899.

and at 5pm two more of the same caliber ... were placed in position.' Napoleon guns joined them, but their movement attracted the full attention of the Confederate artillery: 'The moment their presence was observed, the enemy opened with eight guns; continued an incessant fire for some thirty minutes; then, having a caisson exploded, ceased.' The Confederate guns withdrew behind Benner's Hill to shelter from the larger caliber and greater range of the accurate Union counter-battery fire. This did not really add up to the convincing diversionary action Lee's simultaneous plan called for.

At about 6pm 2nd Division's 1st and 2nd Brigades were ordered from Culp's Hill to strengthen the Union left, which Maj.Gen. George Meade believed to be seriously threatened. A request from Williams to retain at least a division had been overruled and only Brig.Gen. George S. Greene's 3rd Brigade and one regiment from II Corps, scarcely 1400 men, were left. Greene wrote: 'We remained in this position with occasional firing of the pickets until 6.30pm, when the 1st (Williams') Division and the 1st and 2nd Brigades of the 2nd Division were ordered from my right, leaving the entrenchments of Kane's Brigade and Williams' Division unoccupied on the withdrawal of the troops.' Colonel David Ireland's 137th NY Volunteers were initially positioned in the trenches

they had dug about half way along the line on the eastern side of the hill. In Ireland's own words, they '... remained there until about 6pm, when I received orders to send out a company of skirmishers ... At the same time we were ordered to change our position to the line of works constructed by General Kane's Brigade, to occupy which we had to form line one man deep ... In this position, the right of our regiment was entirely unprotected.' Greene was forced to spread his men to cover virtually three times the area he should have covered.

This drastic reduction of Union strength on Culp's Hill is often described as a blunder. This would be fully justified if the position had fallen. But a fairer judgement is that Meade took a calculated risk, encouraged by the apparent reluctance of Maj.Gen. Edward Johnson's II Corps to mount a serious attack on this very strong position. His short internal lines of communication were added insurance.

NIGHT ATTACK: 7PM–12AM

The Confederates finally decided to attack at about 7pm, quite possibly having heard the sounds of the withdrawal of a large proportion of the defending force. They now outnumbered the Union defenders four to one. Light was failing as they moved through the woods to Rock Creek, intent on crossing and sweeping up the slopes of Culp's Hill. Behind trees,

boulders, and from the shadows on the other side, musketry shattered the dimness, sending Confederates diving for cover. Greene had immediately sent out 200 men from the 78th New York to double the strength of his skirmishing screen, which slowly withdrew up the hill. Both the steep hillside and thick woods and boulders, and the knowledge of what the deepening shadows concealed, slowed the advance to a crawl. They were fired upon first from ahead, then their right, their left, and occasionally up the slope from behind. Every Southerner who fell made his comrades move more cautiously. What could have been a ten minute charge to the crest took nearly an hour.

Greene takes up the narrative: 'We were attacked on the whole of our front by a large force a few minutes before 7pm, the enemy made four distinct charges between 7 and 9.30pm, which were effectually resisted. About 8pm the enemy appeared on our right flank and attacked the right flank of the One hundred-thirty-seventh regiment New York Volunteers. Colonel Ireland withdrew his right, throwing back his line perpendicular to the entrenchments in which he had been in position, and presenting his front to the enemy in their new position.'

Colonel Barnum of the 149th NY Infantry described the more stable situation in the main part of the line: 'My command was second from the

---

Items a, b, and c respectively depict Greene's 3rd Brigade flag, the 2nd Division flag, and the corps standard for XII Corps.

a

b

c

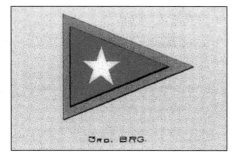

right of our brigade. A substantial breastwork of stones, logs, rails, and earth was hastily constructed, and the regiment rested in its rear until about 6.45pm, when the enemy drove in our skirmishers and attacked us in large force. The enemy made repeated and desperate charges upon our position, but was as often repulsed with great slaughter to him until our ammunition gave out, when we held the position with the bayonet and such limited firing as could be made with the ammunition of the killed and wounded.'

However, the situation was critical on Greene's right where Col. Ireland and his 137th were desperately resisting a powerful flank attack at the point of weakness he had already identified. Brig.Gen. George Steuart's Brigade was threatening to roll up the Union line from the lower end of Culp's Hill which would in turn have exposed the flank and rear of the Union's centre facing north and west on Cemetery Hill and Ridge.

There was a good deal of confusion in the darkness and the Confederates were cautious in their awareness that they were converging from points of the compass, from northeast to southwest, and in danger of being caught in their own crossfire. In daylight they could have seen how wide the intervals were between men and units, and how shallow the Union defense was. In the dark, they saw none of this, nor could they be sure of the positions of their friends. So Ireland, though almost surrounded, was able to retreat to a stronger position where a short traverse ran

The Confederates attack. While Greene's stretched centre held off the frontal attack, his right was outflanked through the space he was now unable to cover. Ireland swung the 137th NY back onto the traverse and, rapidly reinforced, was able to stabilise the situation. If this had been a daylight action the Confederates could well have pushed through to the Baltimore Pike and presented a much more serious threat to the overall Union position.

west from the southernmost point of Greene's original sector.

At about the same time he was joined by reinforcements sent by Maj.Gen. John Hancock from his centre on Cemetery Ridge, rightly concerned that the earlier call for reinforcements had left Greene in a dangerously weak position now that he was seriously under attack. Other reinforcements arrived from the north end of Culp's Hill and one more regiment from the centre. Finally, when the fighting was almost over for the night, the two XII Corps brigades that had been moved to the south of Cemetery Ridge, and had only been involved in the tail end of the fighting there, came back to find their original positions in Confederate hands. After some exploratory skirmishing in this

sector, both sides settled down for a short and uneasy night. This had been rather more than a diversionary action.

MORNING, 3 JULY

On reporting at midnight, Williams had been given a straightforward and predictable order by Maj.Gen. Henry Slocum, his commander: 'Well, drive them out at daylight.' The next three hours were spent in planning for this and positioning his forces, XII Corps artillery in particular. For Ewell and Johnson the objective was equally straightforward, to exploit the previous day's gains and play their part in Lee's unchanged overall plan by pressing the Union's right while Longstreet resumed his assault on Cemetery Ridge. Ewell reinforced Johnson's division and the Stonewall

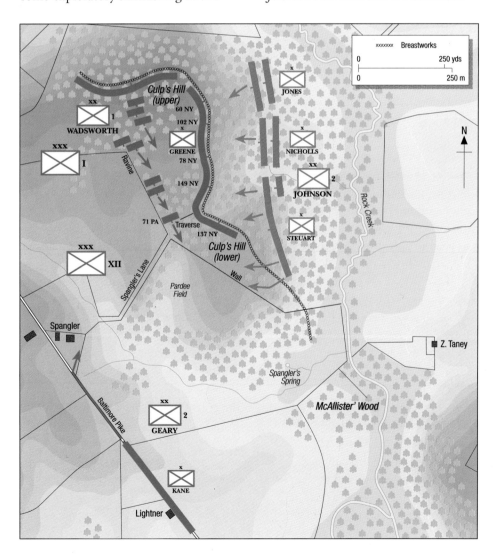

Culp's Hill showing tightly packed trees and the damage inflicted by both Union and Confederate artillery.

Brigade also rejoined it during the night, more or less doubling its strength. However, though pushed back on the line of Spangler's Lane southwest from the traverse at the bottom of Greene's sector and down towards the Baltimore Pike, the Union position was little weaker and now more strongly manned than it had been the previous afternoon. And the Pike itself was strongly defended.

Johnson was ready to attack all along the line with probably the best expectations for success at the southern, lower end of the hill. But the Union actually opened proceedings at 4.30am with an intensive barrage from batteries positioned to the west of the Baltimore Pike and due south on Power Hill and McAllister Hill. Leaving aside some 'friendly fire' damage, Muhlenberg's report that his gunnery 'was of essential service, and did excellent execution' was fully justified. This was sustained for most

of the next six hours and the Confederates could not respond.

Through the morning the Confederates made three attacks on Greene's line and at some points a few men actually reached it, but each attack ended in failure. Between attacks sniping fire was continuous.

Greene fully exploited the advantage of his position pouring fire into the oncoming Confederates. When his units tired, ran low on ammunition, or their rifles began to overheat, he sent them behind the lines to relative safety while fresh troops moved into the trenches. A soldier of the 137th New York, Ireland's regiment, wrote, 'just back of the breast work was a hollow where the reinforcements stayed. A regiment would use up their ammunition in about two hours, when another one would relieve them and they fall back to the hollow where the balls would whistle over their heads. They would clean their guns and get some more

ammunition and be ready to relieve another regiment. They would all rather be in the trenches than in the hollow. In this way we could have stood as long as the rebs chose to show themselves below, which was until 11am, but few were seen after this.'

Johnson's first two attacks had been direct assaults up the hill from Rock Creek. His third and final attempt on the position combined a repetition of the first two with a move against the lower southern part of the hill. The Stonewall Brigade, right of the line, took on Greene's center and Brig.Gen. George Steuart's brigade advanced to the northwest to assault the line at Spangler's Lane. Brig.Gen. Junius Daniel's Brigade was to advance on Steuart's right and link with the Stonewall Brigade. It was observed that both Steuart and Daniel 'strongly disapproved' of the plan. The major commanding the 1st Maryland Battalion on Steuart's right regarded it as, 'nothing less than murder to send men into that slaughter pen'. The attackers on the eastern side of the hill at least had the benefit of patches of cover and shelter from artillery harassment

Steuart's Brigade had to leave the protection of the captured trenches and make its final advance, mostly in the open across the Pardee Field, into a crossfire of artillery and musketry, and was shattered. Was this the real blunder of the battle?

Daniel's Brigade made some slight impression on the Union line but had to withdraw when its left was exposed by the evaporation of Steuart's Brigade. Brig.Gen. James Walker reported laconically that his Stonewall Brigade had met with 'equally bad success as our former efforts'. Solid volleys broke them up. A few made it to within 15 yards of the breastworks and one sergeant died on the parapet in an attempt to take the colours of the 149th New York. After an hour or

The fighting was so intense that four years later a visitor to the north-east slopes of Culp's Hill found the trees 'completely riddled' by musketry with most of the largest girdled and dead from the shock.

so Walker withdrew: 'as it was a useless sacrifice of life to keep them longer under so galling a fire'.

CONCLUSION

Johnson made no further attempt on this Union bastion: 'All had been done that it was possible to do', he wrote: 'The enemy were too securely entrenched and in too great numbers to be dislodged by the force at my command'. But Steuart's success the night before had marked as much of a high-water mark as Pickett's charge would later that day. Ewell's diversion had turned into a series of major but ultimately fruitless brigade and divisional actions, and cost the Army of Northern Virginia 2000 or more killed, wounded, missing or captured. Union losses totalled a few hundred, the majority, 300, in Greene's brigade, which had the largest share of the action and had crucially held fast at the moment of crisis when night and the hill were their only allies.

SUGGESTED READING

Arnold, James and Wiener, Roberta, Order of Battle 6: *Gettysburg 2 July 1863 Confederate: The Army of Northern Virginia*, (Osprey, 1999)

Arnold, James and Wiener, Roberta, Order of Battle 7: *Gettysburg 2 July 1863 Union: The Army of the Potomac*, (Osprey, 1999)

Coddington, Edwin B. *The Gettysburg Campaign: A Study in Command*, (Charles Scribner's Sons, New York, 1968)

Pfanz, Harry W., *Gettysburg: Culp's Hill and Cemetery Hill*, (University of North Carolina Press, Chapel Hill, 1993)

Scott, Robert N., LTC. *The War of the Rebellion: A Compilation of the Official Records of the Union and Confederate Armies*, Series I, Vol. XXVII, Part I Reports, (Government Printing Office, Washington, 1889)

Smith, Carl Campaign 52: *Gettysburg 1863*, (Osprey, 1998)

ABOUT THE AUTHOR

Carl Smith resides in Virginia with his wife and family and is the author of several books on both the American Civil War and World War II.

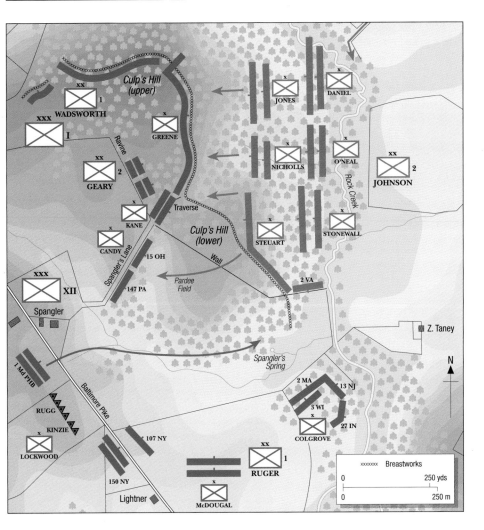

The pattern of the three attacks through the morning of 3 July. During the first attack the 1st Maryland (Potomac Home Brigade) attempted to recover the lost ground between the Confederate left and the Spangler's Spring marsh but were not supported and had to fall back. In the final attack Steuart led his disastrous charge across Pardee's Field whilst the Stonewall Brigade made no more impression than the previous attacks on Greene's solidly defended entrenchments.

The Roman Invasion of Britain

NEIL GRANT

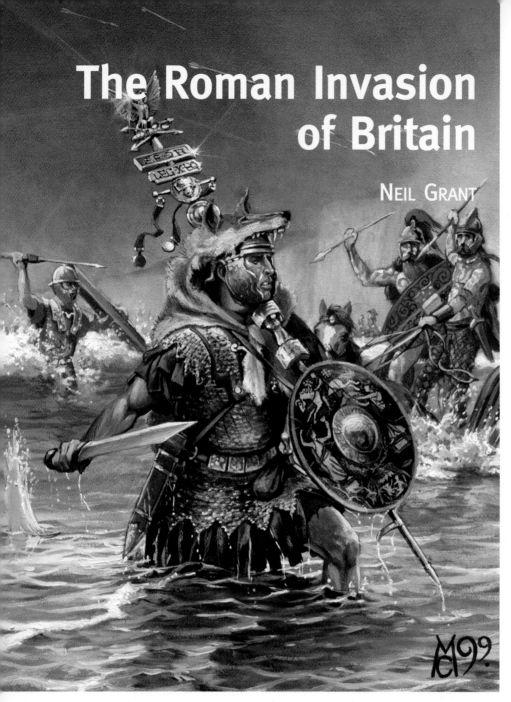

'The Eagle Attacks' – an aquilifer from Legio X 'Equestris', 55BC. This famous incident from Caesar's earlier invasion of Britain only serves to highlight the disparity in information available about the two invasions. ('The Eagle Attacks' copyright Mark Churms 2000/thehistoryweb.com)

The invasion of Lowland Britain by the Romans in AD 43 is one of the most significant events in British history. For the English at least, it marks the very beginning of history, when for the first time events were recorded by residents, rather than foreigners depending on hearsay and rumour. Histories of England traditionally start with the Roman conquest. The date may be less universally memorable than the Norman Conquest of 1066, the only other successful military invasion of Britain, but it marks an equally significant historical milestone.

Based on major archaeological excavations over eighteen years, it has long been accepted that the Roman landing took place at Richborough in north-east Kent.

Since the 1930s, virtually all books on the subject have treated this as established fact. Recently, though, a challenge has been sounded from the vicinity of Fishbourne, the grand Roman villa, now more appropriately described as a palace, in Sussex, above Chichester Harbour and about 150 miles along the coast south-west from Richborough. The Sussex archaeologists claim that the continuing excavation of what had been regarded as a minor supply base, possibly connected with the invasion or its immediate aftermath, was in reality something much larger – nothing less, in fact, than the site of the main invasion.

Less is known of the events of the Claudian conquest than of the two expeditions of Julius Caesar in 55 and 54 BC, for which we have the soldierly account of the commander-in-chief himself. The only substantial description of the invasion of AD 43 is that of Cassius Dio, in his history of Rome written over 150 years later but bearing evidence of acquaintance with earlier sources now lost.

The expedition consisted of four legions plus auxiliaries, probably about 40,000 men altogether, under the command of Aulus Plautius, governor of Pannonia. It sailed from Boulogne and landed almost unopposed. After several skirmishes, the Romans reached a large river where the Celtic tribes assembled to contest their advance. A great battle ensued and the Britons were beaten. Aulus Plautius advanced to the Thames, where he won another battle, but having lost a lot of men in the Thames marshes, decided to wait for the arrival of the Emperor Claudius, bringing reinforcements that included those great frighteners of ancient warfare, elephants. Now led by their emperor, the Romans continued their advance on their objective, Camulodunum

(Colchester), the stronghold of their chief opponents, the Catuvellauni. Claudius remained long enough to see Camulodunum fall and, according to the inscription on his triumphal arch in Rome, to accept the submission of eleven Britannic chieftains (including one alleged to have come from the Orkneys). He departed only 16 days after he had landed. These latter events are well attested, but for the actual invasion and its immediate aftermath, virtually the only evidence is that provided by Dio or by archaeology.

Dio does not say where the Romans landed, nor does he name the river where the great battle took place. Nineteenth-century historians speculated on various possibilities, but the most likely landing place was always Richborough, in north-east Kent, known to be the port of entry for Roman supplies during the subsequent, ongoing conquest, and the site of a victory monument erected soon after AD 80. From there to a point at which the Thames could be forded (possibly between Westminster and the City of London) the natural route was parallel with the Thames estuary, perhaps along the track of the future Roman road (Watling Street), fairly close to the coast. In that case, the large river must have been the Medway at Rochester or, more likely, a few miles upstream, where a large stone monument commemorating 'the Battle of the Medway in AD 43' was erected as recently as March 1998.

This scenario was apparently confirmed by the archaeological excavations at Richborough from the 1920s. They revealed, below later Roman buildings, substantial defensive ditches and a supply base dating from the early Claudian period. Some rather slight evidence to support the battle on the Medway

Detail from Trajan's Column showing Roman legionaries fighting the 'barbarians'. (German Archaeological Institute, Rome)

turned up in 1957 with the discovery of a cache of coins, the latest dating from AD 41, at Bredgar, some miles east of the Medway. It has been tentatively assumed to have been stashed by a Roman officer killed in the subsequent battle – though if that is so, the officer concerned must have been a man of remarkable prescience to anticipate the battle when still the best part of a day's march away. But even without the Bredgar hoard, the Richborough-Medway thesis seemed beyond doubt. So the books have said since the 1930s, and so, on the whole, they still do. But in the last few years a shade of doubt has appeared. Some have mentioned the possibility that one division of Plautius's forces may have landed in the west, though they still maintain that Richborough was the main site.

In spite of the hectic pace of archaeology, the case for the Solent as the site of the Roman invasion, first proposed in a scholarly journal ten years ago, rested mainly on

reinterpretation of the historical evidence rather than on new discoveries, and to a large extent it still does.

Aulus Plautius assembled his forces, Dio tells us, at Boulogne in the spring of AD 43. Sailing was delayed by a mutiny: the soldiers were unwilling to venture forth upon the Ocean, regarded as the boundary of the inhabited world. An emissary had to be summoned all the way from Rome to stiffen their backbones, so the delay must have been considerable, long enough, apparently, for the Britons, who of course knew what was afoot, to have relaxed their guard on the south coast and returned to their farms.

At sea, Plautius divided his force into three. It was once assumed that there were landings at Dover and Lympne, besides Richborough, and that the three divisions later linked up somewhere near Canterbury, but no archaeological evidence of landings at Dover or Lympne, nor of a sizable base at Canterbury, has been found,

Reconstruction of a 'Fulham' pattern sword and scabbard, named after an incomplete specimen recovered from the river Thames. (In the collection of Mr T. W. Rath, Vermont, USA)

and it may be that the division of the fleet was just a temporary diversion intended to confuse watchers on the shore. The next incident, as reported by Dio, has been seized upon as ammunition for the Sussex school. The ships were guided, he says, by a shooting star, which moved from east to west. If they did indeed follow the course indicated by a comet, the Romans could hardly have ended up in east Kent. A landing in the Solent (almost due west from Boulogne) would be more likely.

The Kentish riposte draws attention to the powerful westward trend of the current and the prevailing westerly winds in the English Channel, which would tend to impel the primitive Roman vessels towards the Kent shore. Moreover, Caesar, who also embarked at Boulogne, landed on the beach near Deal, only a few miles south of Richborough (had he known of the natural harbour at Richborough, he would no doubt have made use of it: his unprotected achorage twice brought him close to disaster). Finally, the Kentish men add, it is abolutely unheard of for anyone planning to invade southern England, including Hengist and Horsa, Napoleon and Hitler, to contemplate landing anywhere except Kent (though William of Normandy bent the rules slightly by landing over the border in East Sussex). There are indeed several strategic reasons why Kent should be favoured, not least that it is closest to the European mainland. The crossing from Boulogne to the Solent is about twice the distance from Boulogne to Richborough.

It is generally accepted that the prime reason for the invasion taking place when it did was the desire of the newly annointed Emperor Claudius – whom even his own family considered something of a wimp – for a great military triumph. But the official reason was a worthier one. It was to restore Verica, the refugee king of the Atrebates, to his kingdom, from which he had been driven by the encroachments of the Catuvellauni. Had the Romans been NATO, the spin doctors would have described the operation as one of liberation rather than conquest. In fact, one contemporary scholar, amiably tossing a spanner into the works, has recently suggested that, since southern Britain was already so Romanized, it was perfectly natural for the inhabitants to look to Rome for relief from a native aggressor!

The political situation in southern Britain was fluid, ill-defined and remains, to say the least, obscure; but it revolves around the ascendancy of the Catuvellauni. Their homeland was, roughly, Hertfordshire, north of the Thames, but by 43 they were dominant throughout most of south-east England. It is likely that their expansion began under Cassivelaunus, Caesar's chief opponent. Part of the agreement with Cassivelaunus that concluded Caesar's campaign in 54 BC promised security for the Trinovantes of Essex, who had sought Roman aid against the aggression of their Catuvellauni neighbours to the west. Nevertheless, the rise of the Catuvellauni continued, notably under Cunobelinus, or Cunobelin (Shakespeare's Cymbeline), the length of whose rule, nearly 40 years, alone, attests to unusual capacity. In AD 5 or soon after, the Catuvellauni took over the Trinovantes' oppidum at Camulodunum, which became their own 'capital'. They absorbed several small tribes, on both sides of the Thames, and dominated larger ones. Suetonius's description of Cunobelin as *Britannorum rex* was not unreasonable (Cunobelin's son Caratacus, in flight after the Roman victory, apparently had no trouble in establishing his leadership over the Welsh tribes to continue resistance to the Romans).

There is no reason to assume (though many do) that this ascendancy of the Catuvellauni was inimical to Rome. Caesar, after all, was long dead and with him the Roman obligation to the Trinovantes, while Cunobelin's relations with Rome, commercial and diplomatic, may well have been perfectly satisfactory to both sides. However, in 41 or 42 Cunobelin died, and his inheritance was divided between two sons, Togodumnus and

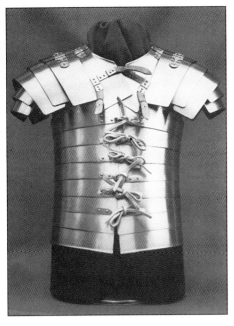

Reconstruction of a Lorica segmentata found on the site of the Roman supply base of Corstopitum, near to Corbridge in Northumberland. (In the collection of the Lancashire Schools Museum Service)

Caratacus, wild, headstrong young men who lacked their father's moderation. One immediate casualty was Verica, ruler of the already much diminished territory of the pro-Roman Atrebates, which spanned the Sussex/Hampshire border. Driven out, he sought refuge in Rome. Earlier displaced Britannic kings had followed the same course, but none had succeeded in securing active Roman intervention on their behalf. But Togodumnus and Caratacus were bold enough to demand Verica's extradition and, when this request was ignored, caused 'disturbances', presumably armed raids, on the coast of Gaul. This furnished the reason, or the excuse, for the Roman invasion.

The territory of the Atrebates was a long way from Richborough. On the face of things, a landing in the Solent would have made more sense, as it would have taken place on Atrebatic territory, although it is not certain that the Romans' reception would have been friendly even there if the Atrebates had been conquered. Verica himself disappears from the

story; we do not know if he was restored or not, but if he were he died very soon afterwards. His successor, Cogidubnus (possibly the instigator of Fishbourne palace), remained a firm Roman ally for the next 30 years.

However, the ultimate Roman objective was not to rescue the Atrebates but to crush the power of the Catuvellauni princes. That was best done by an attack on their power centre – Camulodunum – and for that purpose, says the Kent school, a Richborough landing, and a route following that pioneered by Caesar, was the sensible option. Thanks to the proximity of the coast and the Roman command of the sea, maritime support could be utilised practically the whole way.

Whether the scene of the Roman advance was Kent or Sussex, the evidence suggests that Roman operations afterwards shifted westward, to Dorset and the Isle of Wight. This could be an illusion, arising partly from the fact that the division involved in that area was the Second Legion (Legio II Augusta), whose commander was the future emperor Vespasian; his exploits naturally engaged the attention of later writers. He is said to have fought 30 battles against the Britons,

The possible routes taken by the Roman invasion force in AD 43. (© Copyright Osprey Publishing)

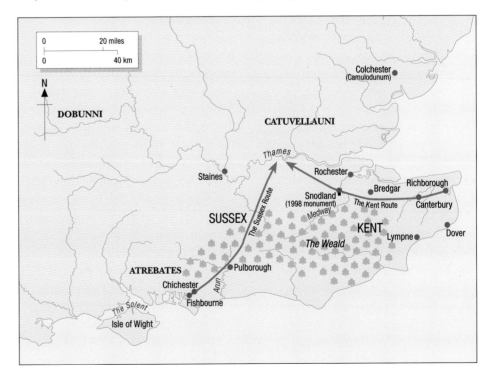

The grave stele of Marcus Favonius Facilis, a Centurion of the XXth Legion, killed during the invasion of Britain in AD 43. (Colchester Museums)

he was probably the victor over the Durotriges of Dorset, and the conqueror of the great hill fort of Maiden Castle, near Dorchester, where startling evidence of the fierce fighting has survived in a Celtic skeleton penetrated by a Roman bolt. On the basis of a remark by the 4th-century historian Eurotropius, that command of the invading army was shared between Plautius and one Sentius Saturninus (not mentioned by Dio), it was suggested many years ago that Saturninus might have commanded a subsidiary division, which landed in the eastern Solent to secure the kingdom of the Atrebates. But the presence of the Second Legion in Dorset and the Isle of Wight in late AD 43 or, more likely, the following year, in itself cannot be taken as evidence for a landing in the Solent.

Clearly, the route taken by Plautius's army to its undisputed destination on the Thames is a crucial question. Archaeological evidence is very scanty (it is worth remembering that in spite of assiduous searching for evidence of Caesar's movements in Britain a century earlier, not a trace of them has been found), and what little there is, such as the Bredgar hoard, can be interpreted in more than one way. On the central issue – the identity of the river where the two-day battle was fought – we are thrown back on Cassius Dio.

The river, says Dio, was so formidable an obstacle that the Britons believed the Romans could not cross without a bridge (they were wrong; some aquatically skilled German auxilliaries swam across fully armed and took them by surprise). Clearly, then, this was a large and strong-flowing river. Dio also implies, though he does not actually state, that the river was fairly near the Thames. His description fits the Medway perfectly well.

There is no river of comparable size to the Medway on the route between the Solent and the Thames. The Sussex alternative is the River Arun, with modern Pulborough as the tentative site of the battle. Today, the Arun at Pulborough hardly looks likely to hold up a troup of Boy Scouts, let alone a Roman army, but it still occasionally floods even now, and in the 1st century it would have been unchannelled, forming a floodplain over half a mile wide (easily conceived from a viewpoint on the stone bridge at Pulborough today). The Arun is, though, a very long way from the Thames.

In the argument over the identity of the river, the stronger argument seems to lie with Kent (the county was known to the Romans as Cantium, which incidentally is a name, as the Sussex school points out, that is never mentioned by Dio although it was employed by Caesar). Another incident, occurring before the river battle, appears to favour Sussex. After the early skirmishes, in which both Togodumnus and Caratacus were separately defeated, Plautius received the support of 'a group of the Bodunni'. This tribe is otherwise unknown, but it is quite widely agreed that they were the Dobunni, Dio having perhaps confused their name with that of the current ruler, Boduocus. The Dobunni were a large tribe who had also suffered under Catuvellauni hegemony (the 'group' of them who approached the Romans may have represented an unconquered section of the tribe), but their territory was centered on Gloucestershire, far away to the west. It is very suprising to find them seeking out the Romans in east Kent, still less likely that Plautius would, as Dio says he did, despatch a force for their protection. On the other hand, the Dobunni were neighbours of the Atrebates, south-east of them, and, if the Romans were present in Atrebatic territory north of the Solent, Boduocus' eagerness to come to terms with them is understandable. It is difficult to see how this incident can be explained to fit in with the Kentish approach unless the presumption that the Bodunni were the Dobunni is incorrect. But if they were actually a small Kentish tribe that has otherwise escaped notice, why should Dio bother to mention them?

The distance to the lower Thames from Fishbourne is, as the crow flies, slightly less than the distance from Richborough, but that does not necessarily mean that the route taken was shorter. Roman armies, as we know, liked to travel direct, and took pride in demonstrating their supremacy over Nature, no less than over lesser human beings, by overcoming natural obstacles on their way, sometimes building bridges far more massive than needs warranted. But they were not so foolish as to march straight over or through an obstacle if there were an easier way around it, or to ignore an established track because it meandered. The countryside of southern England is hardly rugged but in the 1st century, besides the rivers and some steep slopes, it contained another barrier to an invading army: the primeval forest.

The Weald, an Old English term for forest, stretched across south-east England from eastern Kent to the Sussex/Hampshire border, a dense and roadless forest, a soggy wilderness of thick and thorny undergrowth, of rotting timber and swamp … or so the Kent school sees it.

A line from Fishbourne to the Thames around London passes through the Wealden Forest for up to about 30 miles. For an army carrying vast quantities of baggage on wooden-wheeled carts, says the Kent school, the forest must have been impenetrable. On behalf of Sussex, it must be admitted that we cannot be certain exactly how serious a barrier the forest presented. Evidence of pre-Roman settlement in the Weald is slight, but was it really trackless? In view of the quantity of cross-Channel commercial communication in the century before the invasion, it is possible – highly probable, according to the Sussex school – that a trackway through the forest already existed. And, of course, the Romans overcame much greater obstacles than this. Given time, they would drive a road through the Weald (Stane Street, which recent research has shown extended south of Chichester to somewhere very close to Fishbourne).

The famous 2nd century mosaic of Cupid on a dolphin, situated within Fishbourne Roman palace. (Fishbourne Roman Palace/Sussex Archaeologial Society)

In AD 43 the time was not available, but if it is assumed that the forest was indeed as formidable as it looks from Kent, could they have gone around it? Might they not have outflanked the forest to the west? This would have required a long, strategically undesirable, and perhaps dangerous diversion, say the Kentish men. Yet the diversion need not have been so very great, perhaps only twenty miles or so, and since it would have been largely through Atrebatic territory, it is not obvious where the danger of it lay.

The main objection to the Richborough site has long been that the defensive ditches, traced for about 600 metres and certainly dug about AD 43, enclosed far too small an area for the invasion force. The area appears to be about four hectares (ten acres), about half the size to be expected for even a single legion. However, Brian Philp, director of the Kent Archaeological Rescue Unit, who has been actively excavating Roman sites in Kent for

more than thirty years, has recently resolved this apparent problem. His work at the Roman fort at Reculver, constructed about AD 210, demonstrates that almost a mile of land to the north has been removed by coastal erosion in succeeding centuries. Similar if less dramatic erosion is clear at other sites in Kent, notably at Richborough itself. There, half the large mansion built about AD 100 has been washed away, and even the eastern quarter of the great stone fort, built about AD 279, has gone; the remains of its great east wall now lie on the beach below the eroded cliff. Indisputably, substantial erosion has taken place at Richborough, and the original defended area was almost certainly far larger. Projecting the lines of the ditches, Brian Philp has tentatively identified a rectangle at least 600 metres square (36 hectares or 90 acres). That is easily large enough to accomodate the whole invasion force, and is close to the Wantsum Channel, which divided the Isle of

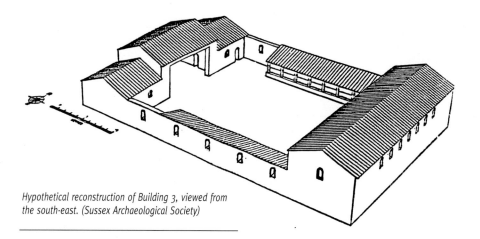

Excavations at Fishbourne Roman Palace 1995 to 1998

Hypothetical reconstruction of Building 3, viewed from the south-east. (Sussex Archaeological Society)

Thanet from the Kent mainland and could have provided safe anchorage for Plautius's fleet.

At Fishbourne, the situation is rather different. The shoreline of Chichester Harbor, and even the stream that runs past the Roman palace (though its course was diverted slightly by the builders of the palace), appear to have changed little in the past two thousand years. The Fishbourne site was first excavated in the 1960s under the direction of the present professor of European archaeology at Oxford. Some remains of military structures of Claudian date (i.e. predating the palace) were found then, but all the interest centered on the magnificent Roman palace with its astonishing mosaics, the finest Roman site in Britain. In the early 1990s, projected highway construction to the east of the palace prompted hasty digging of trial trenches which revealed evidence of Roman structures. Excitement mounted as, beginning in 1995, there emerged the foundations of a very large building. The depth of the foundations suggest that it was of stone, not timber, construction, and it is now tentatively identified as a military principia, a major

headquarters. Obviously, no such building could have been built at the time of the invasion; 'Building 3' at Fishbourne is assigned to the decade beginning AD 50 and may be slightly later than that. However, it was preceded by another – timber – building, of which, unfortunately, most traces were obliterated during the construction of Building 3 but which can be dated to about the time of the invasion (methods of archeological dating, in spite of the near-miraculous advances of recent years, cannot locate a structure within a particular year, nor, except in special circumstances, within less than four or five years).

The issue remains undecided. The argument and – more importantly – the digging continues. Deep in the saloon bars of old Kentish pubs, where you cannot raise your head for fear of cracking it on a beam, you may, in the long summer evenings, hear the rumbles of conspiracy theories. Is it a coincidence, murmur the Kentish men over their glasses of dark ale, keen to stimulate the interest of the innocent investigator who has just bought them a pint, that recent publicity about the Fishbourne site almost coincided with an

application for a grant from National Lottery funds by the Sussex Archaeological Society?

We may never find the answer, but – who knows? – decisive evidence could yet turn up. Perhaps someone will discover an inscription that will provide unarguable proof, one way or the other. Not long ago, in a deep chamber at Fishbourne, thought to have been a treasury, a large and promising stone slab was found. It was face-down and, before turning it, the directors of the excavations had the foresight to set up a video camera to capture the momentous event. The slab was blank.

Meanwhile, perhaps the most reasonable conclusion is a compromise, dividing the honours as evenly as possible between Kent and Sussex. Might it not have been the case that the main army, under Aulus Plautius, landed at Richborough, and the expedition of the Emperor Claudius, arriving only a few weeks later, landed at Fishbourne? Or, indeed, vice-versa.

The author wishes to express grateful acknowlegment of the advice and assistance, sometimes on site, of several scholars, in particular Brian Philp, director of Kent Archaelogical Unit, and David Rudkin, director of the Roman Palace at Fishbourne.

SUGGESTED READING

Rankov, Boris, *Guardians of the Roman Empire*, (Osprey, 1999)

Simkins, Michael, *Legions of the North*, (Osprey, 2000)

Simkins, Michael and Treviño, Rafael, *Caesar's Legions*, (Osprey, 2000)

Wicox, Peter, *Barbarians Against Rome*, (Osprey, 2000)

ABOUT THE AUTHOR

Neil Grant is the author of many books on history for adults and children, and is probably best known for accounts of the history of exploration. Recent publications include an Illustrated History of 20th-Century Conflict; his children's books include the award-winning Children's History of Britain, as well as books about the Greeks and Romans, Famous Battles, Conquerors, etc. He was formerly a teacher and an editor and now lives in south-west London.

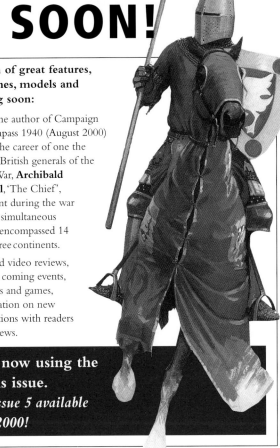

Roman Food and Drink

RENÉ CHARTRAND

BREAD SHOP

What would Claudius's legions have eaten and drunk on campaign and in their barracks? According to Simon Macdowall in Warrior 9: *Late Roman Infantryman 236-565 AD* (Osprey), the daily ration of a legionary in Egypt was three pounds of bread, two pounds of meat, two pints of wine and one eighth of a pint of olive oil. From Michael Simkins in Men at Arms 46: *The Roman Army from Caesar to Trajan* (Osprey) we learn that legionaries carried grain, ham and cheese, and other foodstuffs collected by foraging. None of the literature talks in detail about army catering, but surviving Roman writing about food describes many dishes that are as likely to have featured in a legionary's diet as in a civilian's.

Apicius *On Cookery* (*de re coquinaria*) is the best known and most complete source that has come down to us. It is, in fact, a collection of recipes from several generations of the same family, but the first and best known Apicius, Marcus Gavius, lived in Rome in the same century as Claudius's invasion of Britain. He was a renowned chef and gourmet, and had his own cookery school.

INGREDIENTS

The recipes in Apicius include some rather extraordinary imperial court dishes involving such delicacies as camels' feet, cocks' combs and unmentionable parts of pigs, male and female. But there are also many other everyday recipes which make us realise that Romans ate a lot of pork, fish, chicken, and also small birds like thrushes and larks, still popular in Italy today. For vegetables, leeks and onions were much used. Peas, beans and lentils are often mentioned, also green vegetables, garlic, asparagus, cucumber and gourds. Early varieties of today's European fruits were widely cultivated, as were olives, for eating separately or as an ingredient in many dishes and for oil.

Olive oil was used in almost every dish (never butter). Their cuisine was one of the many elements of Roman culture with origins in Greece, and Eastern influences can be clearly identified in Greek cuisine. Even for basic dishes Roman recipes generally require complex blends of every imaginable spice found between Hadrian's wall and Persia. One finds black pepper, cumin, lovage, coriander, dill, mint, aniseed, saffron, oregano, to name a few, sometimes all in one recipe or even in one sauce! Interestingly, garlic doesn't feature as much as one would expect.

Honey and vinegar were regularly used, often together for a sweet-sour effect. But the most distinctive flavouring ingredients were *garum*, a salty fish essence, and two sweeteners made from grapes, *possum* and *defrutum*. Of all Roman ingredients, garum is surely the most intriguing. It seems to appear in almost every dish and sauce.

The recipe for garum may be a little offputting. Its base was anchovies, left to ferment in brine for some weeks. A liquor was extracted and flavoured with different herbs and spices and

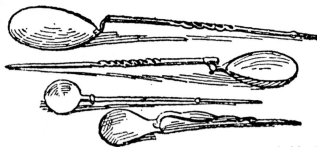

SPOONS

defrutum or possum. We are told there were many different flavours of garum made in both homes and factories (the furthest north found near London) throughout the empire. The end result was an intense salty, fishy sauce which would keep for many months. It is very likely that most legionaries carried a small personal flask in their kit with their bronze cooking pot and other necessities.

Incredibly, something very similar (perhaps even a descendant or ancestor) is still made in South East Asia. It is called *Nuoc Mam* in Vietnam, *Nam Pla* in Thailand and is obtainable from oriental groceries; ask for 'fish sauce'. The English cookery writer Katie Stewart gives a simple recipe which serious gastronomic re-enactors may like to try. However, starting from first principles with a heap of fresh anchovies in hot sunlight is not recommended, having been found to be both risky and antisocial!

You will need:

Salt, ½ pound
anchovy filets
oregano, one teaspoon
6 tablespoons of defrutum

Bring to the boil in 1½ pints of water and cook briskly for about 15 minutes. Cool and strain three or more times through muslin till fairly clear. According to one scholar the result should be 'of murky colour, salty taste and pungent aroma'! This can be bottled and will keep for several weeks.

For the less adventurous there are various anchovy essences and pastes to be found in European and American delicatessens.

Possum was raisin wine. Italian Vin Santo is probably the nearest present day equivalent, but sweet sherry, madeira or vermouth will give the right effect. Defrutum was a reduction of must and can be made by boiling red grape juice down by about two thirds.

PANIS

Roman bread was made from various sorts and qualities of flour, much as today, but did not rise much. Barley bread was eaten as well as wheat, though the former seems to have been regarded as a punishment in the army. Loaves were usually round and dented on top so they could easily be broken into four, six or eight pieces. Roman soldiers on campaign would be issued with hard, twice-cooked loaves, which would keep for many days. Unleavened bread was also eaten and would have been very much the same as today's pita bread.

VINUM

What wine did our Roman legionaries and their officers drink? What wines should we serve with our re-enacted cookery? This is an enormous and complex subject. The legionaries' basic drink was actually vinegar mixed with water, but a lot of wine was also drunk, and ale in Britain. Roman wine may generally have been sweeter and heavier than most wines today and would often have been cut with water. So, to suit modern palates, but to maintain a link with the ancient past, I have selected some good Italian wines that are made from ancient grape varieties. These were introduced into southern Italy by the Greeks with such success that the area became known by the ancients as *Enotria*, 'the land of wine'.

The best-known of these grapes was called *Gemini*, 'Twins', from its double branches. It is still cultivated today and is now called *Greco*. Greco di Tufo should certainly be on the wine list. It is a distinctive white wine, quite full and brisk, and makes a wonderful companion to any of the recipes above. Fiano de Avellino, also from Campania and made from an ancient Roman varietal, harder to find, is even better. The vineyards of Antonio Mastroberardino, produce this fine wine and specialise in production from the ancient grapes found in the region. Mastroberardino has been called the 'wine archaeologist' for good reason!

For the finest red, get some Taurasi if you can find it, also produced by Mastroberardino. It is made from the ancient Aglianico grape and its quality

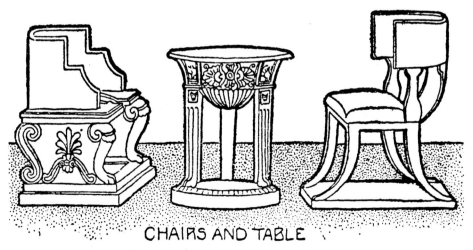

CHAIRS AND TABLE

RECIPES

I have selected and tried out some of the most simple recipes with pleasing results. It should be noted that Apicius leaves the cook to decide on quantities and whether to use fresh or dried herbs, and generally encourages improvisation.

BOLETUS

For four, you will need:

Mushrooms, up to a pound (*the wide-capped variety is best*)

Black pepper, a quarter to half a teaspoon

Lovage (*the pale green leaves of celery are a good substitute*), half a teaspoon

Honey, one teaspoon

Vinegar, one teaspoon

Garum, one teaspoon

Olive oil, two teaspoons

Slice the mushrooms. Grind the pepper and chopped lovage with a pestle and mortar (or in the blender) with the rest of the ingredients. Cook gently all together over a low fire for five minutes, until tender but not too soft. Dried boletus mushrooms (ceps) will take about 40 minutes. Serve hot or cold with stone-ground wholemeal bread.

PORRUS

Leeks make another very simple starter dish.

To serve four you will need:

Leeks, about 1½ pounds

Olive oil, two tablespoons

Garum, one tablespoon

Red wine, half a glass

Boil the leeks in water with a pinch of salt and a little olive oil until tender but with a little bite. Drain, slice lengthwise and put in a dish. Pour on the garum, olive oil and wine mixed up as a vinaigrette. This also may be eaten hot or cold with bread.

CUNICULUS

This recipe was a particularly good find. Fresh rabbit, probably trapped on a foraging expedition, would have made a nice change from the salted or smoked pork which the legions marched with. The recipe demonstrates both the complexity and the simplicity of Roman cuisine. The complexity is in the list of spices and herbs; the simplicity in the ease of preparation. The result is a surprisingly luscious dish. This is also a good way of cooking chicken, but rabbit works best.

For four, you will need:

One rabbit

Olive oil, one tablespoon

Garum, one tablespoon

Stock or broth, a good pint

Two or three leeks

Coriander, a pinch

Dill, a pinch

Joint the rabbit and brown it in a small amount of the oil. Add the rest of the oil, the leeks sliced into fine roundels, garum, coriander and dill. Pour on enough stock to cover the meat (this can be chicken stock if you don't have enough rabbit to enable you to make broth from the bonier parts with leek, onion and herbs). Cover and cook at a low simmer for an hour or so until tender. Reduce or drain the cooking juices, depending on how much liquid you want.

While the rabbit is cooking, prepare the sauce using a typically Roman variety of ingredients:

Pepper, a pinch

Cumin, celery and coriander seeds, a good pinch of each

One medium onion, finely chopped

Parsley, mint and fresh coriander, enough for one teaspoon of each when chopped

Garum, one teaspoon

Honey, one teaspoon

Vinegar, one teaspoon

Juice of half a lemon

Defrutum or possum, one glass

Flour, one tablespoon (*optional thickening*)

Using a mortar and pestle, crush and mix all the spices and herbs. Add garum, honey and some of the cooking broth as you go along to make a smooth paste (making a curry involves the same sort of process). Put the paste in a small pan and mix in the lemon juice, vinegar and defrutum. Bring to the boil. Reduce the heat add the flour to thicken (if you wish). Pour over the rabbit and serve.

PERNA

Finally, a recipe for boiled ham, most likely a staple item in the legionaries' diet. The Romans used dried figs to soften the salty taste of their ham or bacon and this certainly works well with today's meats. The result is a juicy and deliciously simple dish.

You will need:

Ham, gammon or bacon leg (*preferably smoked*)

Dried figs, two or three per pound of meat

Bay leaves

Put in a pot and cover with water. Bring to the boil and then simmer for 90 minutes or more depending on weight. Drain (discarding the figs) and allow to set for a few minutes before slicing and serving hot or cold. Shredded cabbage can be added for the last 10-15 minutes of cooking, a one-pot strategy which would have appealed to legionaries.

Apicius went on to criss-cross the fat with a knife and fill the cuts with honey. He then rolled the ham in a paste of flour mixed with olive oil and baked it in a medium oven for about 30 minutes until nicely browned. But this is a fancy variation which legionaries would probably not have bothered with. Another variation, which I favour, is to push figs into deep slits cut into the ham before cooking.

The leeks and mushrooms will go well with this, as with the rabbit.

Cuniculus

is so good that some call it 'the Barolo of the South'; it should not be drunk young. Another very good red is Aglianico del Vulture, slightly lighter in character, but whose long and robust taste should satisfy the most discriminating modern-day legionary; look for the Riserva which will have been aged at least five years. For a more ordinary but pleasant red, try Lacryma Christi del Vesuvio in the amphora-shaped bottle which recalls its ancient origin, though the Romans certainly did not call it by that name. Mastroberardino, again, makes the best.

Would good Italian wines have been available in the farthest reaches of the empire? Certainly – communications were excellent and amphorae (large clay wine jars) holding about 35 litres and sealed with a large cork covered with wax were used for storage and transport. As they were completely airtight, the wine would keep well, good ones for up to twenty years. Moreover, to maintain the legions' rations and supply the colonies, new vineyards were planted as the empire advanced north, up the Moselle near the great fortress town of Trier and in Gaul in the areas now known as Provençe, Bordeaux and Burgundy – some of Rome's great contributions to our civilisation!

FURTHER READING

Andrew Dalby and Sally Grainger, *The Classical Cookbook* (British Museum Press, London, 1996) gives excellent background, translations of several Apicius recipes and mouth-watering interpretations for the modern cook. The Roman section of Katie Stewart's *Cooking & Eating* (London, 1975) is also informative. *Apicius: Cooking and Dining in Imperial Rome* (Dover Publications, 1978) is a fuller translation of *De re coquinaria.* A French work, *À table avec César* by Pierre Drachline and Claude Petit-Castelli (Paris, 1984) is also highly recommended. For scholarly detail refer to Williams, Harvey and Dobson (Ed's), *Food in Antiquity* (University of Exeter Press, Exeter, England, 1995).

For ancient wines, see Hugh Johnson's *Story of Wine* (Mitchell Beasley, London, 1998) and Jancis Robinson, *Vines, Grapes and Wine* (Mitchell, Beasley, London, 1985).

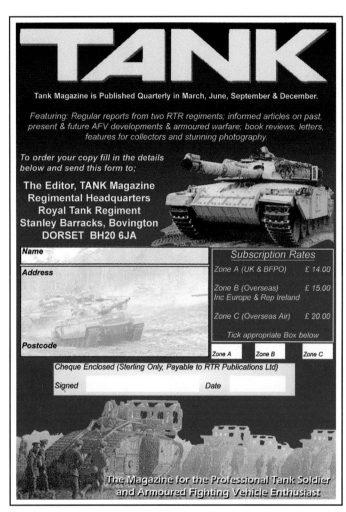

THE MESSENGER

JULY HIGHLIGHTS

**MEN-AT-ARMS 341:
BRITISH AIR FORCES
1914-18 (1)**
The first of two volumes planned to detail the birth of the British flying services, and their baptism of fire in WWI. Offers extensive coverage of a range of air force uniforms and insignia.
48pp • July
• £8.99 / £14.95

**MEN-AT-ARMS 342:
US ARMY OF WW2 (1)
PACIFIC**
Launching a three-volume mini-series studying the US Army's considerable involvement in WW2. The US contributed more men and materials to the war than any other Western ally, and US troops bore the brunt of the fighting in the Pacific theatre.
48pp • July • £8.99 / £14.95

LOCKHEED SR-71
Paul F Crickmore, the recognised world authority on the SR-71, reveals the secrets of the aircraft following its declassification. Now available in paperback.
280pp • July
• £18.99 / $26.95

NEW FROM OSPREY MASTERCLASS

**WORLD WAR 2 LUFTWAFFE
FIGHTER MODELLING**
Essential modelling tips and techniques that perfectly complement the array of historical reference material already available to modellers of this period.
128pp • July • £19.99 / $29.95

QUALITY • ACCURACY • DETAIL

AUGUST HIGHLIGHTS

**COMMEMORATIVE
60TH ANNIVERSARY
EDITION - NEW IN
PAPERBACK!**

SPITFIRE - FLYING LEGEND
A celebration of the most famous combat aircraft of all time, the Supermarine Spitfire, that became a national hero in its own right in the Battle of Britain in 1940.
192pp • August • £14.99 / $19.95

WARRIOR 26: US PARATROOPER 1941-45
The US Paratroopers of WW2 were indisputably some of the toughest, most determined soldiers of their time. Find out what made them so special - how they trained, fought and lived during the war years.
64pp • August • £9.99 / $16.95

**AVIATION PIONEERS:
LOCKHEED'S
BLACKWORLD
SKUNKWORKS**
A definitive pictorial overview of the conception, design and deployment of three of Lockheed's truly pioneering aircraft.
112pp • August
• £10.99 / $16.95

**CAMPAIGN 73:
OPERATION COMPASS**
This British 'Blitzkrieg' saw Lt. Gen. Richard O'Connor's troops sweep 500 miles across the African coastline, destroying 9 Italian divisions and taking 130, 000 prisoners in the course of just two months.
96pp • August
• £11.99 / $18.95

**COMBAT 19:
SUNDERLAND
SQUADRONS OF WW2**
'The Flying Porcupine' with its 14-gun armoury was an immediate success in battle, and helped repulse the German U-Boat menace.
112pp • August
• £12.99 / $19.95

**CAMPAIGN 72:
JUTLAND 1916**
Controversy surrounds Jutland, the only major fleet engagement of WWI. The British public was disappointed by Jellicoe's performance, but he left the Germans with no chance of winning a surface battle.
96pp • August
• £11.99 / $18.95

**CAMPAIGN 75:
LORRAINE 1944**
Revealing Hitler's secret plans to cut off the US Army in the Lorraine, and providing the first ever published account of the decisive encounter at Arracourt.
96pp • August
• £11.99 / $18.95

**COMBAT 20:
TBD DEVASTATOR
UNITS OF THE US NAVY**
Designed as a new torpedo bomber, the Douglas TBD Devastator's only real taste of action came in the pivotal Battle of Midway.
96pp • August
• £11.99 / $17.95

NEW TITLES IN THE ORDER OF BATTLE SERIES

**ORDER OF BATTLE 8:
THE ARDENNES
OFFENSIVE - V PANZER
ARMEE CENTRAL SECTOR**

**ORDER OF BATTLE 9:
THE ARDENNES
OFFENSIVE - VII US CORPS
AND VIII US CORPS
CENTRAL SECTOR**

The second pair of volumes in the Ardennes series, detailing the action in the key central sector of the front from the Allied and then the Axis perspective.
96pp • August
• £12.99 / $21.95

AVAILABLE THROUGH OSPREY DIRECT (SEE OPPOSITE) OR THROUGH GOOD BOOK AND HOBBY STORES

VISIT OUR NEW WEBSITE! www.ospreypublishing.com

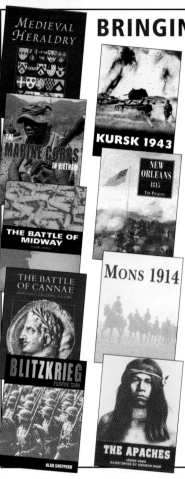
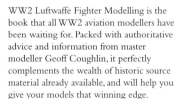

Reviews

Great Military
Blunders.
Six programmes
(three seen) by
Darlow Smithson
for Channel 4,
February/March 2000
and a book, 192
pages, illustrated in
colour and black
and white,
Macmillan/Channel 4
Books, London,
£18.99.
ISBN 0 7522 1844 1

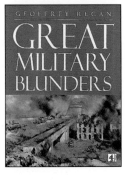

The exploration of the subject involved, it is said, the participation of more than 200 experts. Of these some are identifiable as they are quoted in the text and appear in the television programmes where they have valuable things to say, mostly in general terms rather than as specific observations on the events under consideration. Thirty-four of these experts are listed on the back of the book jacket. The twenty-three histories are supported in the book by twenty-four references (of which three are to works by the same author) and a further reading list of fifty-two books (of which nine are by the same author). At this point a certain unease starts to creep into the observer's mind.

Of the events under examination I have detailed knowledge of a few, superficial knowledge of some and no knowledge at all of others. On the treatment of these last I cannot comment, but my confidence is influenced by the way the others are handled. Sir Redvers Buller is offered, once again, as an example of, in the words of the publisher's copywriter, 'the most incompetent general of the Boer War.' The examination is based on a lengthy essay on his earlier career and a brief and superficial account of the Battle of Spioenkop. This limits the evidence against Buller in South Africa to six weeks' activity, up to the end of January 1900. It omits the operations in the final break-through to the relief of Ladysmith, characterised by Field Marshal Lord Carver as equal to the finest artillery and infantry actions of the Second World War. Also omitted are the successive actions conducted by Buller in northern Natal and in the Transvaal, on the basis of which the American commander of the Boers' Irish Brigade, Colonel J. Y. F. Blake, later wrote: 'The Boers generally acknowledge General Buller as by far the ablest commander the English had in the field. True it is, he made mistakes on the Tugela ...' The sad thing is that here is a lost opportunity. The question of value is what changed between December 1899 and February 1900? How did Buller overcome his mistakes? But that would not be amusing.

What of the presentation? The book has a large number of illustrations that give no relevant information, although the more recent events are better handled. The captions are frequently unhelpful, frivolous or misleading. The pictures do cheer up a typographic design apparently intended to repel people who want to read the words. The opening page of each section is set with a line length more than twice the optimum for comfortable reading and thereafter the type size is dropped to a level requiring 20/20 vision and good light, but mercifully in a serif face. The television programmes have too many instances of visual humming, those images put in because there's nothing else they can think of showing. An umbrella and bowler hat on a hatstand represents the work of a civil servant, for example. This was used when the examination of aerial photos to check the effectiveness of World War II bombing was under discussion; it would be more interesting to see examples of the photos than studio props. Otherwise the production values of both book and television are of a high standard.

The outcome of all this is that good questions are asked, but not answered. The underlying weakness of the approach is that it demands single-cause explanations for complicated chains of events, and that is unrealistic. Intellectual enquiry is too often sacrificed to the wish to create a stir and the slick jibe replaces the considered evaluation. The book and the programmes are very entertaining and enjoyable, but history they ain't. By all means let your curiosity be aroused, but seek your conclusions elsewhere.
Martin Marix Evans

The Trench (1999),
written and
directed by
William Boyd,
starring Paul
Nicholls, Daniel
Craig, Julian
Rhind-Tutt and
Danny Dyer.
Available now for
rental.

This is the directorial debut of the renowned novelist William Boyd, no stranger to First World War topics. He has touched on the war in his novel *The Great Confession* and his excellent novel *An Ice Cream War* is based upon the war in East Africa. The Trench, unfortunately, is not quite of the same calibre. The narrative of the film follows a small group of men left to hold a front line British trench on the Somme battlefield in the three days prior to the great offensive of July 1916, and the action takes place within the same trench for the entire course of the film until the final scenes portraying the men going 'over the top'. The acting throughout the film is uniformly excellent, with particularly strong performances by Daniel Craig as the regular Sergeant and Paul Nicholls as an innocent 17-year old private, terrified and fascinated by everything around him. The only thing that lets this film down is its lack of scale, placing all the action in the confines of a trench serves to place the emphasis on the characters themselves, but it also dramatically limits the scope and scale of the film, at times it seems more like stage play than a film. This said, The Trench is a genuinely impressive directorial debut from an excellent author.
Marcus Cowper

Dispatch – The
Journal of the
Scottish Military
Historical Society.
24pp. Available by
subscription £12
UK, $24 USA.

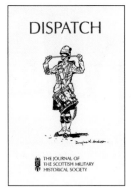

This very creditable journal is issued three times a year to all members of the Scottish Military Historical Society. Its scope is broad but tends to concentrate on the collectible end of the market, covering badges, head-dress, uniforms, model soldiers etc, publishing articles predominantly submitted by members of the society. A typical issue contains articles on the Ayrshire Yeomanry, Sergeant's Dance Kit of the Black Watch, book reviews and even a digest of all the Scottish soldiers in 18th- and 19th-century colonial America, a very useful tool for family historians. The journal is well illustrated, both black and white and colour photography are used throughout, as well as original illustrations. It also has a very lively and informative letters page.

As well as the journal in its printed form the Society runs a web site: http://subnet.virtual-pc.com/mc546367/journal.htm, which carries an index of many of the articles published in the magazine, along with recent research done into Scottish military history as well as a very useful gallery of Scottish uniforms, covering a wide range of units and historical periods. All in all the journal and its website form a valuable historical resource, particularly for those interested in Uniform history, and those wishing to find out more about the Society and its publications should contact Tom Moles, Membership Secretary – SMHS, 4 Hillside Cottages, Glenboig, Lanarkshire ML5 2QY, Scotland.
Marcus Cowper

The Hutchinson Atlas of World War II Battle Plans: Before and After, Edited by Stephen Badsey. Oxford, Helicon Publishing. 288 pages with 42 black-and-white battle plans. £27.50.

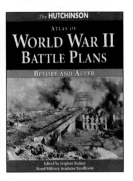

The battles are grouped by threes under seven headings: the Armoured Blitzkriegs, the Amphibious Landings, the Slogging Matches, the Air Power Factor, the War at Sea, the Airborne Assaults and the City Battles. The subjects within these categories are chosen from the war in Europe, Africa, the USSR and the Pacific. Each of the essays opens with a brief chronology, followed by a broad outline of the background and a description of the strategy on which the action was based. Two battle plans, one showing the original concept and, facing it, a second giving the outcome in reality, manage in some cases to give a startling clarity to the story and, even where less successful, are still very useful. A concise account of the progress of the action is followed, as far as is appropriate, by an evaluation of the strategies adopted by the opposing sides. Four or five books are cited for further reading in each case.

Two of the essays are within this reviewer's particular interests. The account of the Fall of France is, overall, excellent. One can argue with some matters of detail, such as the failure to point out the major design faults of the most powerful French tank, the Char B: those of expecting the commander and the driver to double as gunners, the requirement to turn the whole tank to traverse the 75mm gun, and a fatally vulnerable cooling system radiator. It is possible to take issue with comment on the ability of the High Commands of both sides to assess the evolving situation and control their forces accordingly. The castigation of the Allied generalship is entirely justified, but that the German advance succeeded mainly because German attempts from above to slow or halt it failed, could also have been pointed out. These are details that arise precisely because the essay is so useful; the important issues are raised, the tone is cool and critical and rational discussion naturally follows. Much the same applies to the account of Operation Market-Garden in the Airborne section.

The quality of the text is, in general, matched by the quality of the presentation. The line length comes dangerously near, but just avoids, being excessive and the opacity of the paper leaves something to be desired, but the battle plans are admirable and lose nothing by being limited to a single colour. The typography is lively and serves the reader well.

For students of the Second World War, and in particular those interested in the questions of how and why events unfolded as they did, this is a valuable and reliable work, much to be reccommended.

Martin Marix Evans

Waterloo 1815: Les Carnets de la Campagne, published by Editions de la Belle Alliance; No.1 Hougoumont, No.2 Le Chemin d'Ohain, both by Bernard Coppens & Patrice Courcelle. 88 pages, A4 size, card bound; colour & mono illustrations throughout. Distribution by Tondeur Diffusion, 9 Av. Fr. Van Kalken, 1070 Brussels, Belgium. Available by mail order from Librairie Chez Vous, 25 rue Bargue, 75015 Paris, France, price 165 FF each plus 40 FF post & packing.

Can there be anything left to say about Waterloo? Having read these titles – YES. For those who can read basic French, these first two books in a planned series of 12 studies of aspects of the battle will prove hugely rewarding. I don't believe it is an exaggeration to say that they represent the most important original work published on the subject for years, in any language.

Each consists of an account of the events on a particular part of the field, interspersed with lengthy quotations from contemporary reports, memoirs, letters and other eyewitness material, mainly from French and Dutch-Belgian sources (including junior ranks) but also taking British reports fully into account. There are many colour and mono illustrations and maps, including uniform studies of the units involved, pleasingly illustrated by Patrice Courcelle, with useful commentaries. There are also interesting discussions of tactics, central to an understanding of what actually happened on 18 June 1815; biographical notes on the participating commanders; detailed orders of battle, and full bibliographies.

The books' great importance lies in Bernard Coppens' insistence on returning to first principles, leap-frogging over the mass of secondary material published since roughly the 1860s. He records, and tries to reconcile, the earliest and often conflicting accounts by participants – and also shows us the earliest images. These, taken together with the quoted eyewitness accounts, greatly clarify the progress of the fighting between Reille's corps and the Hougoumont garrison, d'Erlon's corps, Picton's division and the British heavy cavalry.

These books are the result of real primary research; they expose many later writings as mistaken (or, like Napoleon's memoirs, a self-seeking pack of lies). I have read at least half a dozen other major books on Waterloo, and thought I had a reasonable general knowledge of the battle; M. Coppens has opened my eyes to the shaky foundations of much of the 'conventional wisdom'. Nobody who has a serious interest can afford to miss this wonderful series; unlike other recent 'revisionist' accounts, which seem to be compiled to fit a personal or partial agenda, these books seek to extend our knowledge based on the eyewitnesses and the documentary evidence. Even at around £20.00 each including postage they are first class value for money. I cannot recommend them too highly. If your schoolboy French is even lying dormant at the bottom of your brainpan, it would be worthwhile making an effort to shake it up again, simply to read these outstanding books.

Martin Windrow

RAF in action 1939-45: Images from air cameras and war artists by Roy Conyers Nesbit. Public Records Office, 256 pp, black and white photography and colour paintings throughout, hardback, £24.99

This volume has covered its broad remit well, and I don't envy the author his task of having to whittle down his photo selection to the 450 images featured within the covers of this impressive illustrated book. Some of the more memorable action shots of World War 2 were taken by aircrewmen wielding a bulky camera in an aircraft that was being shot at by an enemy that they had invariably bombed! These images were crucial for post-mission target damage assessment, and after the war literally hundreds of thousands of photos were given to the Public Record Office (PRO) by the Air Ministry. Few of these arrived at the PRO with any form of supporting documentation describing what they depicted, and it has taken the author many years to sift through the collection and put it in order. The results of his labours are contained within this book, and it is to his great credit that each of the 450 photos boasts a very detailed caption which gives the reader more information than just the aircraft type, target and date. An ex-RAF navigator who saw much action during World War 2 (and no doubt took a few

mission photos himself), Nesbit has drawn on his wartime experiences when compiling this work. From the Battle of Britain to the Dambusters Raid, the bombing of Berlin to the air war in the Mediterranean, all facets of the RAF's war in the air receive coverage. Complementing the photos and captions is a concise, yet informative, body text, which summarises the actions depicted in the images. Also included in the book are over 20 paintings from both contemporary war artists and modern practitioners of the art such as Mark Postlethwaite and Charles J Thompson. I could only find two minor errors in this volume, and both concern the Spitfire. On page 27 the author has not looked closely enough at the Roy Nockolds painting (which is also featured on the dust jacket), for the codes worn by the attacking Supermarine fighters are right for Fighter Command's No. 92 Sqn – QJ, not OJ, as Nesbit opines in the caption! The second error is almost certainly a typo, for the No. 241 Sqn Spitfires on page 193 are Mk. IXs, not 'XIs' – the latter version was, of course, the unarmed photo-reconnaissance variant of the Mk. IX. These are, as I said, only very minor errors, and do little to detract from this highly enjoyable work.

Tony Holmes

Please submit products for review to Marcus Cowper, Editor, Osprey Military Journal, Osprey Publishing, Elms Court, Chapel Way, Botley, Oxford OX2 9LP, UK

History in Action 2000

KIRBY HALL 12–13 AUGUST 2000

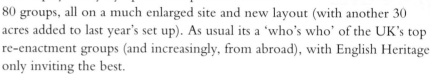

Coming up in August is English Heritage's historical re-enactment extravaganza at Kirby Hall, Northamptonshire. Quite simply, if you are even only slightly interested in history, you have to be mad to miss this event, the largest multi-period historical festival in the world.

Scoring over 99 per cent visitor satisfaction last year, it will be even bigger this August, with over 100 displays a day by up to 3000 performers from 80 groups, all on a much enlarged site and new layout (with another 30 acres added to last year's set up). As usual its a 'who's who' of the UK's top re-enactment groups (and increasingly, from abroad), with English Heritage only inviting the best.

As it's impossible to see everything in just one day, English Heritage strongly recommend a two-day visit. They also warn that due to space restrictions, camping on site is restricted to invited participants only. However, nearby Rockingham Castle will be letting out land for campers and caravan enthusiasts visiting the event.

Participation is by invitation only and if any re-enactment/living history groups not currently on the invitation list would like to attend they should apply to the EH Special Events Unit, 5th Floor, 23 Savile Row, London W1X 1AB with photos, information on levels of authenticity and what they can contribute. Competition to attend continues to be fierce as although a large site, there's a lot to fit in!

The displays will take place within several areas from 10.30am to 5.30pm and the aim is to recreate most eras from the 1st to the 20th centuries. Major displays include;

- Normans and Saxons of 1066 as a taster of this October's massive Battle of Hastings re-enactment (14 – 15 October at Battle Abbey)

- Medieval Jousting and combat displays

- English Civil War battle tactics

- A Napoleonic battle

- The American Civil War (this was particularly popular in 1999)

- The Imperial Roman Army from the 1st to 5th centuries, including EH's latest project, a pair of late Roman cavalrymen using the 'Kontos' – a 2-handed lance at least 12 feet long!

- 100th anniversary Boer War Skirmish (featuring infantry, cavalry and artillery)

- A World War I display, including 3 SE5a biplanes (which may be using part of the site as an airfield, taking off and landing at intervals during the day). If it can be arranged we plan a dogfight with a Fokker Triplane too!

- There'll be a much enlarged World War II battle to commemorate the Battle of the Falaise Pocket in August 1944. This promises to be a real highlight with a 'cab rank' of Spits and a ferocious armoured German counter attack on Allied armour and half tracks.

- A new Grand Finale featuring all participating groups, with fighter flypast.

Visiting families can participate in a variety of activities, including a giant historical dance, or try their hand at soldiers' drill, browse in the large historical crafts market, or take in some of the other attractions;

- Lectures and book-signings by well-known authors, an exhibition of artwork and living history photography

- 'Photos for the Future' exhibition, presented by the History Channel

- An historical fashion show

- Tudor lifestyles, including costume from the Globe theatre

- Wacky comedy (including, we're promised, fleas re-enacting the Charge of the Light Brigade! – music, song and dance of various eras

- The huge range of living history encampments will feature more field fortifications spanning the age

- Talks on arms, armour and many other subjects

- Period food and cooking

- Wargaming, including a participation game

Calendar
Shows and Events

July 1
Wars of the Roses Symposium The Middleham Key Centre, Park Lane, Middleham, North Yorkshire DL8 4RA.
Contact 01969 624 002

July 8-9
ATTACK 2000 Corn Exchange, Devizes, Wilts. For further information contact Stephen Fisher, Belle Vue Villa, Belle Vue Road, Devizes, SN10 2AJ, **tel.** 01380 721683

July 13-16
Origins Game Expo at Convention Centre, Columbus, Ohio.
Information (1) 425 204 2677.

July 13-16
The 6th Annual HobbyTown USA National Convention at the Hyatt Regency, Reunion, Dallas, Texas.
Contact Bob Wilke (1) 402 434 5065 .

July 19-22
IPMS National Convention – International Plastic Modelers Society, USA and North Central Texas Region, Dallas, Texas.
Information (1) 912 922 3918.

July 19-23
The Milennium War and Peace Show. At the Hop Farm Country Park, Beltring, Nr. Paddock Wood, Kent. Open 9am to 6pm.
For further information phone 01622 872068

July 20-23
Historicon. Lancaster Host Resort, Lancaster, PA.
Contact: James E. Thomas Jr. 8314 Sprague Pl., New Carrollton, MD 20784. Information (1) 301 562 4879 Email: kinqit@aol.com

July 27-October 8
Invasion 1066 – Re-enactment and living history events on the Norman invasion and the battle of Hastings, staged by English Heritage at Battle Abbey and Pevensey Castle, East Sussex, weekends, from noon each day.
Information (0)1424 773972, (0)1323 762604.

August 4-6
Model Soldier World Expo 2000 The world's top military modellers. For more information **contact** Mike Davidson, Findon Croft, Findon, Aberdeen, AB12 3RT, UK. Tel. 01224 780606, Fax. 01224 78438 http://members.aol.com/worldxpo

August 6
Sabre 2000 The Pavilions, The Yorkshire Showground, Wetherby Road, Harrogate, N. Yorkshire. 10.00am-6.00pm.
Contact Andy Baxter 01423 541423, www.suc4.demon.co.uk/Sabre/SabreHomePage.htm

August 10-13
GENCON gaming convention at Midwest Express Center, Milwaukee, Wis.
Information (1) 425 204 2677.

August 19-20
British Historical Games Society UK Nationals sponsored by Battle Honours at Loughborough University, 10.00am -5.00pm each day.
Enquiries (0)1372 812132, Email bhgs@netcomuk.co.uk, Website http://www.bhgs.co.uk www.bhgs.co.uk

August 12-13
History in Action – the largest living history festival in the world, staged by English Heritage, Spitfire sponsored by Osprey Publishing, at Kirby Hall, Northamptonshire, 9.30am – 6.00pm each day.
Information (0)1536 203230.

September 16-17
Colours 2000 Wargames & Modelling Fair at The Hexagon, Reading, Berkshire. Email t.j.halsall@reading.ac.uk

October 14-15
The Battle of Hastings, 1066 – Large-scale re-enactment with many other displays, staged by English Heritage, Norman cavalry sponsored by Osprey Publishing, at Battle Abbey, East Sussex from noon each day.
Information (0)1424 773972. English Heritage website www.english-heritage.org.uk